I0027751

# Raising Great Kids in a Chaotic World

# RAISING GREAT KIDS IN A CHAOTIC WORLD

## A Handbook of Strategies, Examples, and Suggestions for Parents and Educators

### ALLEN N. MENDLER

ROWMAN & LITTLEFIELD
Lanham • Boulder • New York • London

Published by Rowman & Littlefield
An imprint of The Rowman & Littlefield Publishing Group, Inc.
4501 Forbes Boulevard, Suite 200, Lanham, Maryland 20706
www.rowman.com

86-90 Paul Street, London EC2A 4NE

Copyright © 2024 by Allen N. Mendler

*All rights reserved.* No part of this book may be reproduced in any form or by any electronic or mechanical means, including information storage and retrieval systems, without written permission from the publisher, except by a reviewer who may quote passages in a review.

British Library Cataloguing in Publication Information Available

**Library of Congress Cataloging-in-Publication Data**
Names: Mendler, Allen N., author.
  Title: Raising great kids in a chaotic world : a handbook of strategies,
    examples, and suggestions for educators and parents / Allen N. Mendler.
  Description: Lanham : Rowman & Littlefield, [2024] | Includes
    bibliographical references and index.
  Identifiers: LCCN 2023036658 (print) | LCCN 2023036659 (ebook) | ISBN
    9781475872316 (cloth) | ISBN 9781475872323 (paperback) | ISBN
    9781475872330 (ebook)
  Subjects: LCSH: Parenting. | Child rearing.
  Classification: LCC HQ755.8 .M4764 2024  (print) | LCC HQ755.8  (ebook) |
    DDC 649/.1--dc23/eng/20230810
  LC record available at https://lccn.loc.gov/2023036658
  LC ebook record available at https://lccn.loc.gov/2023036659

*To my three GREAT adult children, Jason, Brian, and Lisa, who provided the joys and rigors of being a parent, especially for teaching how difficult but necessary it can be to remain calm and thoughtful when you feel like flipping out. Along with your amazing spouses, Ticia, Renee, and Zach, you are raising my eight terrific grandchildren, Caleb, Ava, Meggie, Eli, Brookie, Avi, Noshi, and Cammy, who give me nothing but joy without the rigor. As much as I love you, whoever said the best thing about being a parent is becoming a grandparent got it right! And to my wife and life partner, Barb, who has been there through thick and thin. I am blessed and grateful that you are all in my life!*

# Contents

# Acknowledgments

I'd like to thank my many close friends and neighbors with whom we have shared and continue to share the pleasures and disappointments of parenting. The support we have received and offered has been so important, especially when dealing with difficult situations. While our children are adults with their own families and the issues are different, figuring out when to say something (almost never unless asked) and when to stay silent (almost always) even when we disapprove of their behavior continues to have its challenges. I also want to express my appreciation to the thousands of educators and numerous schools for inviting me to share my ideas and learn from yours about what it takes to be effective while working with difficult students. Given the diversity of your students' backgrounds and experiences, I understand the near-superhuman effort it often takes to show up with your A-game every day. I hope this book will help make your life just a little bit easier in the classroom and/or at home.

# Introduction

This book is a practical resource of tips that parents and educators can individually or jointly use to help kids acquire, practice, and maintain the attitudes, values, and interpersonal skills most children will need to become responsible and successful adults. It is intended as a specific guide educators and other helping professionals can offer parents and other caregivers to successfully navigate the numerous challenges often faced in raising kids to thrive in an increasingly complex, unstable, and unpredictable world. In particular, it offers a wide-ranging array of pro-social and problem-solving strategies such as:

- how to teach the "values" of success,
- how to talk effectively so kids will listen,
- how to anticipate possible consequences before acting,
- how to act responsibly and with empathy,
- what to do when kids push "buttons" (test limits),
- how to equip children with skills they may need if they feel anxious, overwhelmed, bullied, or faced with potential danger.

Although most examples are presented from a parent-child perspective, with minor adaptations such as changing a few words or phrases, educators can apply or adapt most strategies in the classroom or with individual students. In many instances, classroom adaptations are presented directly in the text. Chapter 2 provides educators with effective ways to successfully offer suggestions to parents, including those who may initially be reluctant or resistant to accepting that their child may have a problem or that a different approach may be needed to see improvement.

Some parents are overly anxious and may find calming reassurance in these pages that they are on the right path. My daughter frequently questions her handling of her very bright but "high strung" five-year-old who often has "meltdowns" when he doesn't get his way. In fact, she is very tuned into his need for choices within limits but can become emotionally upset when he does not quickly respond or escalates. Her frustration can lead to self-blame (It must be my fault!), excessive worry (What is wrong with him?), and while rare, even an occasional outburst. Sometimes she will seek and benefit from a different approach, but she mostly needs reassurance that she is on the right track along with a reminder to take a deep breath and an occasional break from him. Many parents and educators unwittingly get hooked into power struggles with their kids and can benefit from an alternative approach to an issue that can lead to a better or quicker outcome.

Some children have issues that may be problematic at school or elsewhere as well as at home (i.e., won't do homework; is quick to anger; gives up easily; struggles socially; doesn't follow rules; pushes "hot" buttons; is often anxious, fearful or stressed; freaks out over relatively minor mistakes and failures). While the context may be different between home and school, when parents and teachers take a consistent approach to an identifiable issue, a successful outcome is much more likely to happen.

The content we explore will enable educators to pass along the equivalent of "best school practices" to parents and can be applied with children at home as well as with students in the classroom to help fulfill the promise of raising great kids to become successful and responsible adults. As well, it is a practical resource child counselors and therapists can offer parents to reinforce insights and new strategies.

## USING THE BOOK MOST EFFECTIVELY

This book is purposely shorter than most. View it as a road map rather than an atlas of what to do and what to avoid doing in situations most parents encounter. For many, this road map will offer sufficient guidance.

If it does not, you may need more personalized help with the assistance of a specialist like a therapist or coach. It is based on having raised three children who are now successful, responsible adults in leadership positions who are themselves parents that seem to be living fulfilling lives while raising great kids.

In the name of full transparency, I have had the good fortune of sharing the role of parent with a partner (my wife) rather than the much more difficult route of having to go it alone. If you are a single parent, I have the utmost respect and admiration for the additional challenges and burdens parenting can present. Just the thought of doing it alone overwhelms me, although I am beyond inspired by the many single parents who have raised and are raising great kids.

Having been a school psychologist for a good portion of my career, I have seen lots of examples of good and not so good parenting and teaching along with the impact it can have. Finally, I am the kind of person who has appreciated getting concrete advice about parenting from those I trust, but at the end of the day I have to do what fits for my kids and me.

There are many examples used throughout the book to illustrate challenges faced by most caregivers along with suggested solutions. If you are a new parent, there are a lot of tips along with examples of how to handle issues you are facing or will for the first time. If you are a parent whose child(ren) nags, whines, throws tantrums, refuses to cooperate, and/or makes poor choices with you, but others like teachers, coaches, and neighbors have nothing but nice things to say, this book should provide some reassurance along with suggestions that may improve things at home. Barring problems to an extreme, its primary benefit may be to help you feel less stressed since the healthy place for kids to be ornery, moody, obnoxious, and defiant is at home. In many instances, kids will save their worst behavior for the people and places that make them feel safest. However, if others are seeing these or similar problems, be open to collaborating with them to explore solutions.

While most content can be applied to children of all ages and cultures, some examples may seem better suited for children who may be younger or older than yours. As such, it may be necessary to adapt a strategy by substituting words and actions that can accomplish the same goal but are a more appropriate fit for your personal or cultural reality. Fill in the mental pictures that depict your own situation(s) and use those strategies that are most relevant to your circumstances.

The same advice goes for teachers. Chapter 3 sets the foundation by exploring what kids generally need from their caregivers along with suggestions about how to meet those needs. Each subsequent chapter tackles a specific issue of importance and provides numerous strategies along with examples about how to use the strategy. To gain maximum benefit, it is best to read the entire book, although you can gain valuable knowledge and skills by reading any chapter without having to read others. In fact, you may find a few ideas in more than one place since some are important to promoting more than one skill or solving more than one problem. Each chapter ends with an opportunity to reflect on what you have learned that can be applied to your circumstances.

## The challenge of change

Despite the best advice and intentions, we will all have moments when we say or do things that we may later regret and want to change. Be patient and kind to yourself. Correct things as best you can and continue to move forward. Don't hesitate to use the three most powerful words when you mess up: "I am sorry." Understand and keep in mind that change is a roller-coaster ride.

Traits and habits are hard to change. Whenever we try to change a behavior, it is typical to revisit the old behavior, sometimes several times, before the new behavior becomes automatic. People on diets will occasionally backslide and eat the forbidden donut. None of us are perfect. Rather than beat yourself up, it is far more helpful to forgive yourself and get back on track. Apply this principle to your kids as well.

Some of the suggested strategies, particularly those designed to improve the behavior of your child, may differ from what you are used to doing. For example, it is quite common for parent-child and teacher-child power struggles to develop a pattern of escalation that results in an unsatisfying outcome. For change to happen, the pattern must be interrupted, which may require a new or unfamiliar approach.

Practicing and then using a new skill several times is the only way to develop a new pattern. With this in mind, first practice and then implement the strategies that you think will best fit your situation at least FIVE times or for a minimum of two weeks before deciding whether or not to continue. An exception is a child behaving recklessly or aggressively. For example, five "warnings" before a different intervention for fighting would be both ineffective and irresponsible.

If you notice even small changes during this period that may be accompanied by backsliding, consider that strategy a keeper and make it part of your "parenting/teaching toolbox." On the other hand, if you notice virtually no change in the desired direction, move on. Some kids and parents may need more intensive support to get on the right track. Don't hesitate to seek or accept help when you feel uncertain or overwhelmed.

# The Challenge of Raising Kids Who Thrive

*We may not be able to prepare the future for our children, but we can at least prepare our children for the future.*
—Franklin D. Roosevelt

At a trip to the zoo with my then two-year-old grandchildren and my weary son (their father) who had just completed a medical residency, I asked him which he thought was more difficult: being a medical resident working ungodly hours or looking after the kids all day. Without hesitation, he said, "The kids. . . . Even though they provide more joy, there is also no rest."

Recently, the same son, whose three children are now in their tweens and teens, said about parenting, "I love my children but I hate being a parent." While I know this is far from his daily sentiment, it was that day's reality. He was referring to the myriad of issues, trade-offs, and challenges that each child brings, sometimes all at once. Among them are:

- What do I do when my kids don't do what I say?
- Which battles are worth fighting and which are not?
- How do I handle things when the kids are constantly bickering with each other?
- Where is that fine line between supporting and spoiling?
- What do I do when it is just *easier* to give in, not *better*?

7

- How do I stay in charge without becoming a mean dictator when my kids are pushing my buttons?
- When do I let my child handle a problem with a teacher or other adult, and when do I step in?
- What should I do if and when other kids are mean to my kid?
- How can I help my temperamental child settle down?
- How much damage am I doing if I do or don't expose my child to every activity imaginable (every item in the curriculum)?
- When should I negotiate vs. tell my child the rules?
- When should I seek professional help?

Based on the sheer number of teachers who are leaving the profession in droves, educators can undoubtedly create their own list. More than one teacher I know has expressed a similar sentiment as my son in reference to teaching: "I love my students but I hate a lot of things that go along with trying to teach them." According to an American Psychological Association survey (McMahon et al., 2022), nearly a third of teachers reportedly received at least one incident of violent threats during the pandemic and almost half said they planned or wanted to quit or transfer jobs.

Sadly, we are currently raising our children in a sharply divided culture of values, beliefs and privilege or lack thereof that too often leads to intolerance, incivility, and violence. And all of this at a time of traumatic upheaval as children, parents, and caregivers are emerging from a pandemic that turned just about everyone's world upside down, disrupting whatever structure and routine a family or school may have had and dramatically changing how, where, and when adults work and children learn. Many more social, educational, and economic changes undoubtedly lie ahead as a result.

Although there is no absolute blueprint for all parents and teachers to follow, this book is about how to equip your child with the tools to become a *successful*, *responsible*, and *satisfied* person in a complicated world. Notice the words "equip" and "tools" because even the best equipped tools must be learned and properly used. Like a master chef who learns how ordinary ingredients must be used in different combinations to achieve a desired flavor, children must learn not just the ingredients of success but how to blend each with others to achieve a desired result.

## What it takes

Ideally, raising great kids starts with expressions of love: a smile, a hug, or when we tuck our child into bed. It starts when we adoringly blow "raspberries" on our infant's stomach, when we act silly together or share a special song. It starts when we celebrate milestones like learning to walk and talk and read and then get along with others. It starts at school when we welcome our students. It continues even when our kids are crabby, cranky, and challenging, yet we remain able to somehow keep ourselves calm as we soothe and redirect them. It continues as we turn away from the natural instinct to protect and keep our kids happy toward realizing that their emotional resilience depends on learning to deal with the bumps and bruises of disappointment and failure.

Striking the right balance between opposing forces, such as when to tell vs. negotiate, indulge vs. earn, support vs. rescue, is an unending challenge for every parent and many educators. How we talk to children, set limits with them, and model the values we want to instill in them greatly influences how successful and responsible they will become. Yet as much as we might want to, it is impossible to get it right all the time. Even if we could, children are separate beings, and while parents and significant caregivers have considerable influence in how they turn out, there are many other factors including *luck* and *temperament* that play a role.

There are examples of great parents and teachers who do all the right things yet their child struggles in life, as well as children who succeed despite poor or absent parenting and teaching. I often ask parents who attend my seminars and have more than one child to raise their hand if one of their children drives them "more crazy" than the others. Virtually every hand goes up.

Parents and educators are usually the first to receive blame from kids for shortcomings but rarely receive praise for achievements until children are much older, if at all. I can attest to this personally. One of my adult children, who is quite successful by virtually any objective measure and with whom my relationship is overall kind and loving, sometimes seriously and other times jokingly attributes all of his negative personality traits to me, but few of his positive ones.

Get good at understanding and "validating" your child, but do not expect reciprocation, especially during the formative years. Even if you become the best parent there ever was, there are guaranteed to be moments when you will need to rise from the ashes of feeling like the worst there ever was! The same can be said for teachers who may occasionally lose patience with students whose needs demand excessive attention.

As you leaf through the pages, keep in mind that raising great kids requires the right kind of effort but does not require perfection.

## QUESTIONS FOR REFLECTION

1. If you could go back in time what would you tell your parent(s) that you most appreciated about how they raised you?

2. Is there anything you would ask them to have done differently?

3. What feedback or advice might you seek from your child's teacher(s) that could be helpful?

4. If you are a teacher, what do you most need from parents to help their child be successful?

5. What suggestions, ideas, or strategies are you hoping to get from reading this book?

# CHAPTER 2

# Tips for Educators When Offering Suggestions

IT IS NOT UNUSUAL AT A PARENT-TEACHER CONFERENCE, OR AT SOME less formal get-together, for parents to share concerns they may be having at home. As most educators know, it is not uncommon for children with behavior problems at school to present similarly challenging behaviors at home. Most parents are therefore appreciative of suggested solutions and interventions. They are usually open to sharing, cooperating, and collaborating. Some are able to offer more effective strategies to the teacher.

However, for a myriad of reasons, there are some parents who feel vulnerable and may initially be reluctant to acknowledge parenting challenges they are dealing with. Some parents may be embarrassed to come across as anything less than a perfect parent. Others may be unaware that their child's educator(s) may be able to help. Some may disagree with certain teaching methods and may not think s/he might be helpful with issues faced at home.

I recently attended a parent-teacher conference during which the mother sat stiffly and silently with her arms crossed. When given an opportunity to share concerns, Mom expressed the belief that her child didn't like coming to school because he felt criticized and embarrassed when he made a mistake reading aloud. Although he was a good reader by all objective standards, he had had much difficulty learning to read in the early grades and began to stutter when he was anxious or unsure. While he had overcome his reading woes, the anxiety and stuttering remained problematic. Mom's sharing led to a good discussion of her child's past and current issues, but some parents silently sit and suffer with their concerns for fear of making matters worse.

Some parents may be reluctant to seek help or accept a suggestion because they think the teacher does not understand or like their child. There are parents who themselves disliked school during their formative years and who prefer avoiding any contact because they carry uncomfortable memories that can be easily triggered. Some are struggling financially and have all they can do to put food on the table, while others are emotionally overwhelmed and hear suggestions as demands. Unfortunately, some people are angry at the world for whatever the reason(s) and school is just one more place to express their dissatisfaction. With some divisive politicians seeking political gain by stoking fears that schools are inculcating values they may oppose, some parents simply don't trust educators.

To counter these trends, lowering parental resistance can be essential in creating a safe space for parents and educators to share concerns and offer solutions that each may find helpful. The following tips can be helpful when you seek to better understand a student from a reluctant, uneasy, or blaming parent's perspective and perhaps help to gain their cooperation:

## ASK—LISTEN—LEARN!

It can really help when parents believe we know, understand, and genuinely care about their child. Early in my career, I met Mr. and Mrs. D at a parent-teacher conference where they quickly came across as demanding, abrupt, and somewhat intimidating. Despite much data to the contrary, they insisted that their autistic and behaviorally challenging daughter with limited speech (Lily) was much more capable of learning and could handle a regular class for at least a portion of the day. Her well-meaning teacher offered a number of sound reasons for why she thought doing so would overwhelm Lily and could create classroom chaos. Although they found reasons to abrasively find fault with the teacher's explanation, their passion and love for their daughter was obvious to me.

Just when things seemed at a stalemate, we began to explore in greater depth why they felt as strongly as they did. Rather than continue to offer explanations for why what they wanted wouldn't work, we began asking questions to explore how it might (Is there anything special about how Lily learns at home that might help us get her to learn more easily at school?). Among other things, they explained how Lily was much better able to remember things when information and directions were sung rather than said.

Their input was instrumental in getting us to realize how powerful music would become in teaching content to her. We began pairing music with familiar tunes when teaching basics as well as more complex concepts. After doing this for a few weeks and realizing that music made a difference, she was mainstreamed for a portion of the day accompanied by a teacher aide and experienced considerable success.

Perhaps at least as important was coming to realize how demanding and stressful life was for these parents in trying to provide for their very needy child. If you encounter resistance, try to defuse by first expressing compassion, and then listen rather than tell. Here are some examples:

*"Ms. Parent, nobody knows your child better than you so I'd like to hear your thoughts about_____and any suggestions you may have."*

*"Knowing how much you love and want only the best for your child, I have no doubt that by working together, we will see some real growth. Tell me your thoughts."*

After listening:

*"Thank you for sharing and I appreciate your ideas."* (agree to try whatever sounds doable for you)

Explore anything important that might be going on at home:

*"Are there any challenges you face at home with (child) that I might be able to help with?"* Or if the parent shared a home concern without being prompted: *"I have some thoughts about what you might say (do) at home*

*that could help. Would you like to hear what they are?"* (offer a suggestion or strategy that fits).

## KEEP THE FOCUS ON THEIR CHILD

It is not unusual for kids to blame someone or something else when things don't go their way. For example, some students complain to their parent(s) that their teacher is "unfair" when they get a lower grade, a different assignment, or are "picked on" more than their peers. If parents take the complaint to the teacher and offer examples to support their conclusion, acknowledge that you often do different things with different students because you want to help each become more *successful* or learn more about *responsibility*. Then invite parents to offer a better alternative if they have one for their child. For example,

> *"Your child is an excellent writer and he is correct when he tells you that he received a lower grade on his essay than some other students whose essays may not have been as advanced. But my goal is for your child to become an even better writer than he already is and his last essay was not nearly up to his capability. As for the grades of others, I don't discuss specifics with other families except to say that showing improvement is a factor in everyone's grade. He knows that he can improve a grade by turning in an essay that shows a better effort. Would you like to know what I am looking for to see that effort?"*

Rather than parents and teachers saying something like "life is unfair so get used to it," the above gives a sensible reason for addressing a child's specific need in a way that may be different than a sibling or student.

## SHARE HONEY BEFORE VINEGAR

It is a lot easier to get parents to cooperate and open up about issues they may have at home when you express how their child is an asset in class, even when the "asset" creates problems for you. For example,

> *"Trevor can be a delight in class especially when he participates in class discussions. He often contributes very well when we have class discussions. Tell*

*me what you think are his best qualities? My challenge is trying to figure out how to best work with him when he doesn't like an assignment. Do you sometimes ask him to do things that you consider important but that don't interest him? How does he react? How do you usually handle those situations and how do things usually end?"*

## Genuinely acknowledge concern

If a parent expresses concern and attributes it to the teacher, be a strong active listener. Then agree that there may be a basis for it (none of us are perfect). Continue by seeking ways for how the parent thinks things might improve and explore whether the suggestion is applicable. For example,

*Parent: "I think he's bored! He says he hates school and you pick on him a lot."*

*Teacher: "I'm sorry to hear that and I'd like to fix that if I can. It is always my goal to have every one of my students feel good about being here and if either you or he has any ideas about how I can make things work better for him and learn what he needs to know, please share your thoughts."*

If suggestions are offered that you consider viable, thank the parent and let them know you plan to try them. If not, let them know why not:

*"As much as I wish I could, here's why I couldn't (wouldn't) be able to do that in my class."*

Conclude by exploring solutions that involve the student and possibly parent(s). For example,

*"Bored or not, I am sure you agree that we need to help Trevor find better ways to express himself so that he will be more successful in school and be seen by others as the really good person we both know he can be. Please contact me if you have more ideas that can make that happen more often."*

## SHARE WHATEVER SCHOOL VALUES ARE CONSISTENT WITH PARENTAL VALUES

Let parents know that there is very little if any daylight between what you and the parent want for their child. With few exceptions, all parents and teachers want their child to be successful, feel safe, and learn both their rights and responsibilities. One of the most effective strategies is to refer to their child as "our child" (i.e., "Sometimes *our child* struggles with his impulse control at school. Is that something you notice at home?"). If the parent shares the same concern, ask what helps at home. If the parent seems open to a strategy that you use, ask, *"Would you like to hear some ideas that you might find helpful?"*

## QUESTIONS FOR REFLECTION

Think of a disgruntled parent(s) who blamed you for their child's poor performance or challenging behavior.

1. How did you react?

2. What did you do?

3. How did things turn out?

4. What strategies or suggestions from the chapter connected for you or might have led to a better outcome if something similar happens again?

5. Identify one or two takeaways you might want to put or keep in your toolbox?

# CHAPTER 3

# What Children Need from Parents and Caregivers

*Your children need your presence more than they need your presents.*
—Rev. Jesse Jackson

RAISING GREAT KIDS IS BEST GUIDED BY A SET OF *VALUES* TO ADDRESS their needs along with lots of *practical strategies* to handle the many big and little challenges life presents.

How do you want your children to be when they are adults? How do you want them to act toward you and others? What values do you want them to acquire? What opportunities do you want them to have? What are the most important things you want them to tell their children that they learned from you? What do you want them to most remember about you?

It is important to ponder these questions since your answers will form the foundation of how you parent and what you teach. My perspective is for my children to feel fulfilled and live a fulfilling life. I want them to think independently but never believe they have all the answers, to feel confident about who they are and their possibilities and humble enough to understand that others with fewer gifts are equally worthy of their respect. I want them to also understand that being the "best" means being their best, which will rarely, if ever, be better than everybody else but will just about always require commitment and hard work and will at least sometimes replace "fun." I want them to make good, morally sound decisions *in my absence* that contribute to making the world just a little bit better. I want them to be able to handle the many difficult emotional and practical challenges that life presents without falling apart. I want them to feel love and be loved but to understand that the world does not revolve around them and that differing views should be respectfully heard. From a practical standpoint, I want them to have a well-enough paying job to comfortably support themselves and their families . . . What do you want for your kids?

In the wonderfully touching book *Big Russ and Me*, a tribute to the love and respect for his father, the late Tim Russert describes one of the biggest challenges he faced as a parent. Referring to his son Luke, Russert tells how he always wanted Luke to know how much he was "loved but never entitled." What does that mean to you?

How many toys are too many? How much praise is too much? How do we acknowledge discomfort without giving in to unreasonable demands or actions? Should an allowance be given or earned? We give our kids a sense of fulfillment not when we do or get things for them but rather when they grow up feeling **connected** (I belong), **competent** (I can do it!), **compassionate** (I care about others) and in **control** (I can make decisions). They should know they are loved (to feel worthwhile) but not owed (to develop humility). Since teaching and responding to the needs our children have is the key to raising great kids, let's look at these more closely:

## CHILDREN NEED US TO TEACH AND SHOW THEM PROPER VALUES

In an era where it seems increasingly acceptable to say or do hurtful things to others we dislike or with whom we disagree, children need parents and teachers to teach and show them positive values like kindness, generosity, thoughtfulness, respect, and non-violence. Healthy values are driven by consideration of how our attitudes and choices affect others. If Nolan sees his dad exhibit road rage when another driver cuts him off, he learns that yelling, swearing, and revenge are acceptable behaviors when angry. If instead he sees Dad talk out his frustration in a spirited way (e.g.,

"Good drivers should be more thoughtful!"), he learns that talking things out can alleviate stressful feelings. If kids hear things from their parents like, "I'm going to whip your butt unless you apologize," they learn that you can get what you want by threatening violence. If we tell them to tell someone who calls that we aren't home when we are, we teach them to lie. When they see us donating our time and/or our money to help others, they understand that giving makes the world a better place.

Children need not only to hear and see us use good manners with others but to experience our use of good manners with them, like saying "please" when we ask them to do something and "thank you" when they do it. It is primarily by watching how their parent(s) interact with them and others that our children learn to internalize the values they live.

Kids may not always listen to what we tell them, but they are constantly watching what we do. Do our words and actions make the world a better place for us and for those who may look different and who may have different beliefs or preferences? Do we remain calm in the face of life's daily annoyances and frustrations or are we quick to beep the horn, swear, and lose our temper when a driver cuts in front too closely? Are we open to improving ourselves by recognizing and working to eliminate whatever biases we may carry?

Other than extremists who blame and marginalize certain ethnic or religious groups for their own failures, most people deny or are unaware of biases they may carry. Several years ago while teaching a course to educators, an African American educator approached me after class and kindly but directly shared her belief that I was racially biased. Taken aback, I tried to remain calm and asked for an explanation. She told me that while demonstrating positive and negative behaviors of grade school students, I was consistently asking participants of color to play the role of a "bad" student and white participants to role-play a "good" student. I might have been doing that long before she pointed it out, but until that moment I had no awareness.

More recently, the Black Lives Matter movement further stirred me to examine my attitudes and behaviors since I have come to realize that my attitude is not always aligned with my behavior. If I want my child to adopt the values I believe are necessary to live a rich, fulfilling life, I must be open to recognizing and confronting any negative stereotypes I may have internalized. We mirror values to our children primarily by our actions.

**Suggestion:** Teach your child to assess what they have to say to someone after they silently ask themselves these three questions suggested by Socrates, "Is it true?"; "Is it kind?"; "Is it necessary?" Children need their parents and teachers to show, model, and expect them to demonstrate appropriate skills, manners, and social graces. The ability to get along with others is almost always identified among the top traits employers want when hiring a prospective employee. Someone with poor social/interpersonal skills needs to not only learn new skills, they must also unlearn those already ingrained. To help our kids be successful, both parents and teachers need to teach and have students practice:

- Making a request—Use "Please" and "Thank you."
- Accepting criticism—Say, "Thanks for the feedback"; "I didn't realize but now I know."
- Saying what you want and what you don't want—Use "Please," "Thank you," and/or "I" messages: "Please don't yell at me when you want me to do something."
- Getting someone's attention—"Excuse me, Mr(s). _____. When you have a moment (sec) I'd like to ask (tell) you something."
- Not interrupting when others are talking.
- When to say please, thank you, and excuse me.
- Using words rather than fists when mad (i.e., "I am really mad right now.")
- Apologizing with words and sincerity (i.e., say how you may have contributed to a problem: "I'm sorry I said some hurtful things"), followed by improvement.
- Waiting one's turn.
- Remaining quiet in certain situations (school, church, etc.).

- Returning borrowed items without reminders and on time.
- Turning off cell phone at school.
- Offering to help someone.
- Writing a thank-you note or making an appreciative phone call when gifts are received.
- Doing the right thing without having to be told.

## CHILDREN NEED TO UNDERSTAND AND ACCEPT THAT THERE ARE OTHER POINTS OF VIEW

There are 350 million people in the United States. With the exception of Native Americans, all of us either came here looking for a better life or are descendants of those seeking greater freedoms and opportunities. Immigrants, many undocumented, continue to flood our borders seeking safety and the freedom to express who they are and pursue what they want.

Our founding fathers wrote a constitution that recognized the limitations of mankind by stating "We the people . . . in order to form a more perfect union." The best they could do to offer their vision of what that *more perfect union* would look like was to state a general set of principles (i.e., establish Justice, ensure domestic tranquility, provide for the common defense, promote the general Welfare). In their wisdom, they must have realized the impossibility of providing guidance for every situation or for knowing what every situation would be.

While blind to their own limitations or biases (i.e., viewing slaves as property rather than people), they clearly wanted a country that would have laws applied equally (establish justice), allow people to live peacefully and get along with each other (promote the general welfare), be safe (provide for the common defense), and be free to think and value one's beliefs (secure the blessings of liberty). Had they known or could agree upon what "perfection" was, I'm not sure they would have left the bulk of the work to Congress, States, Localities, and Individuals (We the people) to define what that would look like. Since then, each generation has been challenged to define, maintain, and re-define the freedoms this brilliant document offers against the issues of the day. to make a "more perfect union."

In our day, one main issue facing parents and schools is deciding whether to teach our kids that families are comprised of lifestyles that may not mirror theirs, who, if anyone should do the teaching and how the information ought to be taught. Another has to do with racism. Most of us know it still exists, but is it "institutional" meaning that it is baked into the fabric of our culture and shapes behaviors even among the unaware or is it largely a relic of the past that some who need a scapegoat hold onto and espouse while others use as an "excuse" for their life circumstances.

**Suggestion**: In a culture as diverse as ours with liberty and lawfulness being of utmost value, don't kids need to learn that you can believe however you want as long as your actions do not harm someone else? Bitter conflicts are avoided when people from different backgrounds, lifestyles, and points of view can allow others to live their lives without fearing harm from others who don't agree? Isn't that what "liberty" is? It is the inability or unwillingness to know, listen, and feel for those with beliefs other than their own that is at the root of the polarization that has divided our nation. Don't we have a responsibility as parents and teachers to shape a more "perfect union" for our kids?

Parents have the right and are going to teach their kids whatever they believe to be right or wrong ("I; We; Our church believe[s]_____ _____"). At the same time, shouldn't parents teach their children that they will meet and have to spend time with kids from other families with other beliefs and opinions who will not think or feel the same way (especially if they attend a public school). How else do we become a "more perfect union" than to acknowledge not only the ugliness of slavery but that some or many believe harmful remnants remain? If we want our kids to have empathy and become tolerant it can actually be beneficial for them to sometimes feel uncomfortable when other lifestyles and opinions of which they may be unaware or that may not always coincide with theirs are presented in schools through books and discussions.

## CHILDREN NEED TO FEEL CONNECTED

Kids thrive when they feel deeply connected to something larger than themselves, such as a family, club, religious community, or school group. It starts at home. There is no greater gift we can give than sharing enjoyable time and focusing on our child's interests and talents. Get comfortable in being around your kids even when they seem uninterested in being around you.

If they seem aloof or self-absorbed, don't take it personally. They usually tell us about their lives on their terms in their own ways when they are ready. By being present, you are likely to be around when the mood to share strikes them. Kids get the important message of belonging when we spend time with them, regularly express our love and affection to them, and show interest in their feelings, thoughts, and opinions.

**Suggestion:** With all of the distractions around us, it can be helpful to set aside specific times for interaction. Some possibilities: Establish a weekly "family-sharing hour" during which all family members get together to express highlights and needs with each other. Teachers might begin the week by giving their students a chance to talk about weekend highlights and disappointments.

- Try to make spending some "unstructured" time with your children a high priority.
- Begin and end each day on a positive note. Show your love through a smile, friendly greeting, listening ear, and hug throughout the day.
- Challenge yourself to spend at least five undivided, uninterrupted special minutes with each of your children every day in which you and they share a highlight of today and a goal for tomorrow.

Teachers are encouraged to identify students who seem disconnected and to spend two minutes with one of them each day in or out of class for a week getting to know each other. Many teachers have found that improving the relationship with a difficult student very often improves the student's attitude and behavior. Parents should make it a high priority to share meals together. There is research that eating dinner as a family an average of five times a week reduces a child's chances of risky behavior. Naturally, this may not always be possible and if it is not, get as close to this goal as you can. Many parents found that eating family meals together was one of the very few benefits provided by the COVID pandemic.

As most of our lives have regained a sense of normalcy, consider at least a once-a-week ritual like Sunday brunch to help develop closeness by defining a time of togetherness without other distractions. Make your house a place other kids want to be; look for opportunities to host get-togethers at your house. If possible, have a play- or game room with age-appropriate stuff that welcomes kids and makes them want to be in your house. Keep some chips and soft drinks handy. Show your face occasionally with a friendly, welcoming demeanor and expressing interest in what they are doing.

Realize that when your house is the "hang-out," you'll know where your kids are and will be able to keep closer tabs on what they are doing.

## CHILDREN NEED TO BELIEVE THEY ARE CAPABLE

While my daughter was participating at a youth event, I was visiting with Beth, another parent who had become a friend of mine through our daughters' various affiliations. We hadn't seen each other in a while and had lots of catching up to do.

Along with Beth was Tim, her younger son looking for ways to alleviate his boredom. To entertain himself, Tim got a ball and began attempting to twirl it on his finger, Harlem Globetrotter style. Unfortunately, he had little success in this endeavor but a lot of desire to continuously show his mother a skill that he had neither practiced nor mastered. Every other minute, Tim interrupted our conversation with a "Look, Mom!" more from an incessant need for attention than an excited feeling of joy connected to improvement. I found myself not only becoming irritated with Tim's interruptions but with Beth's forced patience that feigned encouragement as she smilingly said, "Wow, that's really good, Tim."

I could have forgiven the inaccurate and disingenuous "good, Tim," had she followed that with a challenge (e.g., "Now let's see if you can keep it on your finger to the count of five") or set a limit (e.g., "I'm visiting with Allen now and I'll watch after we finish our conversation. Thanks for waiting").

While children need to believe they are capable in order to approach the world with self-confidence, nobody benefits from false messages of praise. Real self-esteem grows through the mastery of challenge, not by supportive deception that grows a false sense of accomplishment.

Recognize your child's accomplishments, but focus your energy on her *effort* and *practice* as the necessary ingredients for success. As well, challenge your kids to get a little better today than they were yesterday toward the mastery of a skill. For example, "You read two lines yesterday so let's see if you can read the next three today." Help your kids notice the small steps of progress that come with practice and commitment. For example, "I know you've been practicing your shot and you made some baskets today." I believe improvement through effort should be more emphasized at school by allotting it a grade separate from achievement. Some students will never be able to learn as well or as quickly as others. Rather, like a runner who may not win the race but improves his time, a student's improved learning should never go unnoticed even if it doesn't match the norm.

Put your support behind effort. For example, "I can see how much progress you have made and you should feel proud. Last time, you only got five correct but this time you're up to eight. What did you do to improve? Looking back, is there anything else you might do differently next time you study to get an even better result?"

**Suggestion:** The best way to help your child feel capable is by emphasizing the importance of helping others. No matter how difficult one's life may be, there are always others whose life is tougher. When I worked with troubled teens who were incarcerated at a facility for youth, I occasionally brought some of them to my home. Many lacked anything resembling normal family life and I wanted them to experience a taste of what life could be. To my pleasant surprise, I found my own teenage children taking charge of these days by just hanging out, showing them a very different life from theirs, and involving them in activities with their friends. Enriching life for someone else is a great way to enhance a child's sense of competence.

## CHILDREN NEED HELP MAKING GOOD CHOICES AND SOLVING PROBLEMS

In our ever-changing world of technology that emphasizes automation, people will most likely need to learn new skills throughout their lives to stay relevant and employable. Like industrial and warehouse robots that have largely replaced people, driverless cars and other means of transportation will likely soon replace short-haul delivery jobs. Self-checkout counters and stores powered by in-store sensors and facial recognition technology will continue to reduce the need for cashiers. Many restaurants now have self-ordering machines with a few already experimenting with robot-assisted kitchens. It is easy to envision the eventual loss of all jobs that depend upon repetitive performance. By contrast, jobs that require problem-solving, flexible thinking, and creativity will be harder for new technologies to replace, although the applications of AI continue growing exponentially.

We can begin early to prepare our children to rely on their own thinking when parents and teachers seek, recognize, and consider their child's views, actions, and opinions; acknowledge their preferences; and provide choices, especially in mundane activities, like what they do, wear, and eat, and some important ones, such as when to study, which after-school activities to join, etc.

Teachers can do the same by involving them in decisions that directly affect them, such as establishing classroom rules, selecting topics of study, and solving conflicts they may have with each other. When they encounter problems and seek a solution from you, rather than immediately providing one, ask questions that start with some variation of *What do you think might happen if?* to offer guidance (e.g., "What do you think might happen to your chances of making the team if you practice for an extra hour the next two weeks?"; "What are the chances that I'll say yes if you first put your stuff away before asking me if we can go get ice cream?"; "Guess what I'll probably say to you asking for no homework tonight if you complete this assignment right now?").

**Suggestion:** Ask for your child's opinions and encourage independent decision-making around relatively minor issues. Let her be in charge of decorating her room. Seek his opinion when planning a family vacation. Let her choose where to go for lunch, whether to spend free time watching TV or playing a video game, reading this book or that one, ordering a burger or chicken tenders, doing homework now or later. Ask him what consequence he thinks will best teach him that his actions were unacceptable. There are endless possibilities.

## Children need us to enjoy them

We like to be around people who enjoy being with us and so do our children. Play with them. Tickle them. Laugh frequently with them. Let them poke fun at you. Whether you are a parent, teacher, or both, occasionally be silly and act goofy. It is important for children to learn that while life has its ups and downs, there is always room for pure joy. Sadly, many adults neglect nurturing themselves with fun by discounting its importance. In fact, there are now "laughter clubs" in many cities and countries where adults regularly meet to laugh heartily.

Laughter relieves stress, increases creativity, and often helps keep things in perspective. After probably having spent too much time together on a family vacation, I asked my then-eleven-year-old son to remove his coat at dinner in a restaurant. After he didn't comply, rather than back off and be okay with him deciding, I became quickly frustrated, glared at him, and with gritted teeth demanded, "Take your coat off right now!" Both he and the rest of my family froze momentarily with all eyes on me wondering whether they should be fearful or laugh. Realizing at that moment how ridiculous I had over-reacted, I burst into laughter, which they quickly joined. A moment that could have escalated into a power struggle was defused by laughter. Years later, when we get together, we occasionally laugh at the memory and re-visit that incident as a kind of breakthrough that improved our family communication.

**Suggestion:** Look to humor when things get tense: "We sound like a couple of babbling baboons! I bet if we were at the zoo right now, we'd be locked away with them: especially me, but you wouldn't be far behind."

If your child is whining excessively, you might suggest having a whining contest. Ask another family member to judge. Challenge your child to get all whining completed within a minute, and then time it. Complaining usually turns to laughing as both parent and child realize how silly and unnecessary it is to constantly complain. Classroom teachers can use laughter to defuse a tense situation pertaining to conflict with one or more students or to simply lighten the mood during or after discussion of a difficult topic or challenging concept. To prepare, practice quickly bringing yourself to laughter when you DON'T feel like it.

## CHILDREN NEED US TO HELP KEEP THEM SAFE

Children need adults to provide physical and psychological shelter. They need us to provide them with nourishment and direction. Although they may protest, they need us to firmly set limits and be as unyielding as possible when their decisions may lead to unsafe outcomes. For example, even though your kids are likely to balk at a lack of privacy if you monitor their internet usage, they may not understand that decisions they consider harmless can have far-reaching and long-lasting consequences (e.g., "sexting"; bullying; agreeing to meet people they don't know, etc.).

Be sure that privacy settings for the web, Facebook, Instagram, Snapchat, Tik-Tok, and other social media including those yet to be invented are set to levels you are reasonably comfortable with. Just as you should make every effort to know the friends of your child, you should have access to your child's online friends. "Friend" all of them, and be wary of anyone who won't accept your request. If a name is unfamiliar to you, ask your child. You may use this as an opportunity to explain about being wary of or avoiding accepting strangers as "friends," for obvious reasons.

Be aware and involved with Apps your kids are using or are asking for, especially those with live streaming and broadcasting. You can often enable or disable certain features depending on the degree of exposure you are comfortable permitting. To monitor use, you can open a live-streaming account of your own. If you don't know how to set up or use these features, ask around for someone who does. Virtually all social media, including cell phone use has monitoring capability.

While we should respect our child's developing need for autonomy by allowing for privacy, you need to feel comfortable that your child understands potential risks and takes proper precautions. Good parenting is about using accumulated wisdom that keeps our kids safe while guiding them toward making better decisions. From the time children begin communicating online independently, parents and teachers should provide frequent reminders to never send sensitive information online. They must learn that anything they would never want anyone else to see or know about them or about their feelings toward others should not be posted or sent to even their best friend(s).

Since there is a permanent record of everything they send, they should act as if everyone is receiving their information, no matter how private they may think it is.

**Suggestion:** While dining at home with friends one Friday evening, my then teenage son casually announced that his friend was going to pick him up and they were going to a party. As his friend arrived in his small pickup truck, I noticed from the dining-room table, with dinner guests present, a headlight that wasn't working.

I got up from the dinner table, took my son aside, and told him that it was unacceptable for him to ride in a truck with a missing headlight. I offered to drive him to the party if he still wanted to go. Quick to temper, he angrily said he was going with his friend and I couldn't stop him. Blocking the door, I told him in somewhat graphic detail, that although an accident was unlikely, if one happened and he got hurt or killed, I would not be able to live with myself since my grief would be overwhelming. Therefore, he was not going in that truck. Getting even angrier, my son stormed through the house to his room swearing unprintable epithets that ended with him slamming his door shut.

Although feeling embarrassed at this outburst in the presence of our dinner guests, his safety came before everything else. I think deep down my son knew I was right or at least had sufficient respect since he certainly had the strength to push past me if he really wanted to.

Don't be deterred by your child's anger or unhappiness, especially when their immature thinking can have major consequences. They'll get over it. Realize that when you must set limits, try to let your child know how and why their behavior impacts you.

## CHILDREN NEED US TO ENCOURAGE BUT NOT ENABLE

My not-quite-two-year-old grandson is a daredevil. He goes everywhere and tries everything. When he falls or bumps into something, he might cry but quickly recovers and tries it again and again. He requires constant supervision since he knows no bounds and has little appreciation of danger. His mom and dad have their hands full. By contrast, my older grandson's natural inclination is to avoid just about anything physically difficult or unfamiliar. Although curious, sociable, engaging, and very bright, he seems primarily ruled by fear of failure or imagined danger. I have to fight my impulse to give in when he refuses to try or continues to struggle because I adore him and I don't want him to feel uncomfortable. I want to back off and either do it for him or tell him he doesn't have to do it. Admittedly, sometimes my discomfort wins and I do for him what I know he could do for himself. Yet growth occurs by solving problems that feel uncomfortable and mastering tasks that are difficult.

Resist the impulse to fix your child's discomfort. Rather, guide your child to understand the patience that might be needed to solve a problem or to discover whether or not they might enjoy an activity. As a guide, use my "53" rule. Teach your child to try a new activity at least 5 times or for 3 weeks, and a problem-solving strategy at least 3 times before considering a change.

Realistically, acquiring a skill from ground zero requires an ongoing commitment of at least *six months* including a "practice plan." However, after five lessons with practice in between, your child should be showing some self-guided initiative by attending and/or practicing without much prodding from you. If instead, you are constantly reminding or nagging (e.g., "Have you practiced yet?" "Weren't you supposed to work at____?" "You can go play after you practice for a half hour."), tackle the issue head-on ("Even though you [expressed interest; seem to have talent; agreed to try____], I haven't seen you show much enthusiasm for doing what you are supposed to do. I'm thinking that if you wanted to continue, you would look forward to practicing for at least five minutes a day without having to be reminded. Don't you agree?") Keep in mind that most kids will pull away from an activity at least temporarily when something else captures their interest or when they encounter a difficult roadblock.

**Suggestion:** Encourage your child to take at least five sports, music, or tutoring classes before deciding whether or not to continue an activity. Between classes, it may be helpful to develop a practice plan with your child. It will usually take some time for kids who didn't initiate the activity or who don't succeed right away to want to continue.

If you are working with your child to *solve a problem*, explore what she might do to get a better result, and as part of the plan, expect a minimum of three trials before trying something else (e.g., "How do you think your teacher might react if you came on time and asked or answered at least one question every day for the next *three* days?). Three unsuccessful attempts to solve a problem with a specific strategy is usually sufficient before trying something different. For example, if after an invited playmate declines a third consecutive invitation to play, it is probably time for your child to identify another child to invite or activity to fill the time.

The "53" is a preferred method for parents and teachers when there are behavioral issues with a child. Decide on a plan of action, preferably with a child's involvement (implement the plan at least five times or over a trial period of three weeks). If there is some improvement seen within that framework, continue on. If not, move on.

## QUESTIONS FOR REFLECTION

1. What are the most important values you want your children to embrace? Is your behavior consistent with these values? What might you work on to be more consistent with these values?

2. Parents and teachers need to be models of what we expect from our kids, yet none of us are perfect. What are some things you have said or done that you later regretted? Did you apologize? Thinking back, what might you say or do differently if the same thing happened again?

3. To help your child feel capable and able to solve problems, what are some decisions you can leave to your child that aren't dangerous or have long-term negative consequences?

4. Are there any values you support that are different from those at school? In the neighborhood?

5. How could you teach a child to be respectful of values in other places that may be different from those at home (at school)? For example, some teachers express frustration at parents who tell their child to fight if they are being picked on since that behavior is not allowed at school.

# CHAPTER 4

# Paving the Road to Success

*Parents can only give good advice and put them on the right paths,*
*but the final forming of a person's character lies in their own hands.*
—ANNE FRANK

MY MOTHER-IN-LAW USED TO SAY, "ALL THINGS BEING EQUAL, IT'S BET-
ter to have money than to not have it." While I agree with that, not all
things are equal. I have seen many people with plenty of everything
money can buy constantly chasing "more." I have also seen people with
very little materially be more than satisfied than most with what they
have. Real success is about achieving a lasting sense of inner *fulfillment*
devoid of the need to chase "more."

The college admissions scandal involving Hollywood stars and other
high-powered, wealthy people paying big money to get their undeserving
children accepted at prestigious universities was not only very sad and
disappointing, it was stupid, naïve and an example of very poor parenting.
Failing a test or a class, or getting rejected by a top university is not a life
failure, but allowing it to define you as a "flunkie" is. Further, it is far from
certain that there is much, if any, correlation between attending a selec-
tive university and one's degree of economic success (Bouchrika, 2022).
Perhaps more to the point, recent research suggests no difference in job
satisfaction between college and non-college graduates (University of
Notre Dame, 2021). I think it is safe to conclude that however happiness

and education are related, it is much less about where you went and far more about *what you do* with where you went.

Success is achieved by discovering and re-discovering who we are rather than trying to become what others want us to be. It happens when we experience the satisfaction of reaching or exceeding a goal we value that requires effort to achieve. It is when we take possession of our own journey through life by figuring out the gifts we have been given, making the most of those gifts, gaining the strength to deal with setbacks, and letting go of trying to be what we aren't. It's about what we tell ourselves when our effort falls short.

As parents and teachers, our job is to *facilitate* this process, not to *mold* it to our specifications. Children need to paint their own portrait. Good teaching is about providing the best supplies, tools, and lessons we can.

## MAKE OTHERS FEEL SPECIAL

Numerous surveys have found that most employers will expect their new hires to need training in the specific technical skills required for their industry or job project(s). They know they will have to invest a certain amount of time, effort, and money to get a new employee up to speed. These same employers are looking for people who can already work and interact effectively with others. They don't want to spend their time training people who can't get along with co-workers or customers. I believe the best way to prepare our child for success is to teach them how to consistently treat others respectfully.

Take a page from the best leaders of companies with satisfied employees and teachers whom students love. They make everyone from their top advisor to the night janitor feel important and special. For example, they know the names and an interest or two of their people, greet them with a friendly smile, use "please" and "thank you," notice a job well done, and correct mistakes by teaching rather than blaming.

A friend of mine sent an anonymous post from the internet that parents and teachers can use to properly guide children on how to be with others:

*You can't be best friends with everyone, but you CAN:*

*\*Notice everyone*

*\*Be friendly to everyone*

*\*Make room for everyone*

*\*Root and cheer for everyone*

*\*Empathize with everyone*

When your child is in your presence, pay careful attention to show that each person, no matter what they do, where they come from, and how you feel about them deserves your respect. Remember, they won't if you don't! When they talk to Grandma on the phone, remind them to ask, "How are you?" When a spectator praises them for a good play after the game, teach them to make eye contact and say "thank you." Show and teach them that it's pretty easy to make just about anyone feel special with a hi, a smile, and a positive word.

## HELP YOUR KIDS DEVELOP S.M.A.R.T. GOALS

S.M.A.R.T. is an acronym that stands for SPECIFIC, MEASURABLE, ACHIEVABLE, REALISTIC, TIME-LIMITED. The concept was originally developed by George T. Doran (1981) and has since been applied in many settings. Unlike a general New Year's resolution to lose weight, a S.M.A.R.T. goal would be to lose 10 pounds in the next month. A S.M.A.R.T. homework goal for a hyperactive child might be to "write two sentences of five words each or until the timer reaches five minutes before taking a stretch break." A goal for a highly anxious child who is a "perfectionist" might be to "set aside at least a half hour of fun and relaxation every day for a week."

Start with goals that are relatively easy to reach since each small success sets the stage for the next. Involve the child in doing the goal setting. Finally, have your child write down the goal. Studies have found that we are much more likely to achieve our goals when we write them down (Maata, 2023).

## CELEBRATE SUCCESS

When your child is successful, express pride and enthusiasm. Use words or phrases like "Wow" and "Way to go!" Teach your child to savor the small victories ("Doesn't that feel good?" "You worked hard and it paid off."). Perhaps equally important is to avoid giving false praise. Although it has become commonplace for children to get a trophy just for showing up on the little league field or at the dance competition, save your excited praise for the accomplishment of a SMART goal. Humility is learned by not becoming overly enamored with the victories. Wisdom develops by learning from the defeats.

## CHALLENGE NEGATIVE THINKING

Words like "I can't," "I'm unable," and "It's too hard" block success. When you hear these negative voices, teach your child to add the word "yet" or "so far." Then redirect your child's attention, asking him to say, "I haven't YET"; "I've been unable to SO FAR." What we tell ourselves affects how we feel about ourselves. There is a difference between thinking, *I'm stupid* or *I'm bad*, which imply permanent conditions that can't be fixed, and *I haven't figured it out yet* or *I need to try a different approach*. The former leads to a hopeless feeling with no real solution. The latter suggests a temporary problem that has a solution. Quickly follow by helping your child develop a plan to achieve the goal.

## SUCCESS HAS TO BE TASTED BEFORE IT IS DIGESTED

Kids need to taste success to get or stay interested. All it takes for a lousy golfer to come back to play again is to hit one or two good shots. They can be far from perfect and feel successful. There is a lesson there that applies to teaching and parenting. They will not learn or behave if they come to believe that nothing changes no matter what they do.

If a child completes a few chores but they aren't done to your satisfaction, stay away from criticizing that there are still clothes in the corner or crumbs on the floor. Before correcting, genuinely focus on and appreciate what s/he did. Get in the habit of beginning a correction with something that pleased you. For example, "Jon, thanks for following through on making your bed and sweeping the floor. By the way, maybe next time, you can take an extra look to make sure there aren't any crumbs or clothes still lying around. Thanks again." Or, "Samantha, you got the first three correct, which shows a good understanding of how equations work. You are on your way. Now let's look at the next three that gave you some trouble."

## BUILD ON SUCCESS WHEN THE GOAL HAS NOT YET BEEN ACHIEVED

Let your child know that she already has the tools to be successful or simply has to expand upon those already present.

If a person on a diet eats a forbidden pastry, rather than criticizing, it is better to point to the success that preceded the letdown (e.g., "I noticed that the pastry sat on the counter for at least two hours before you gave in and ate it. How did you manage to avoid eating it for all that time?").

When your child struggles, use prior successes to get her back on track (e.g., "I know it is hard to finish the assignment, but there are only three problems left. How have you managed to complete the first six because you weren't excited to do those either, yet you found a way to get them done?"). If your kids are bickering with each other, you might say, "The last time you both wanted to watch different shows, you eventually figured out a solution. What did you do then to stop the arguing?" If no answer, "I remember you agreed to take turns when you wanted to watch something different. Who had the last turn?"

## CONNECT SUCCESS AND FAILURE TO *STRATEGY* AND *EFFORT* RATHER THAN *ABILITY*

Edison failed hundreds of times before he finally figured out how to make the electric lightbulb work. When asked if he became frustrated with the failures, he claimed that he hadn't because each failure eliminated a possible solution and brought him closer to the actual one. He could have given up if he thought he was incapable of solving the problem. Rather, he must have instead concluded after each failure that he had not yet discovered the correct strategy to make it work.

When children are struggling to learn or behave, try to help them attribute their victories and difficulties to *effort* ("I barely studied for the test so I got a poor grade") or *strategy* ("If I took a few deep breaths when I got angry to calm myself, I probably wouldn't have gotten into trouble by having a verbal outburst."). To stay motivated when things aren't working out the way children want, they have to believe they are capable of success but haven't put in enough effort or that they aren't using the right strategy. If, instead, children conclude that they don't have the *ability* to succeed, they are much more likely to give up.

## HELP WITH ORGANIZATION

Some bright youngsters struggle to succeed because of poor planning and organizational skills. They may seem to always procrastinate, be forgetful, appear unmotivated, or even come across as oppositional. Instead, many have a hard time sequencing and/or remembering that most tasks have a series of steps that need to be done in order for a task to be successfully accomplished.

These kids often have trouble seeing the big picture. For example, they may misjudge that competing with an assignment due next week is a music lesson, sports practice, a busy weekend, and studying for a math test. So instead of beginning it now while they have some free time, they either wait too long to do a good job or completely forget about it.

Help your child establish routines, priorities, and timelines. Make a daily schedule with your child that identifies activities and time slots.

Teachers can help by providing students with two different colored folders—one for completed assignments and the other for incomplete assignments. S.M.A.R.T. goals will also help (e.g., "Before I watch TV, I'll put all the stuff I need for school tomorrow in my backpack.")

## Identify a "suck it up" timetable

When our son was struggling in sixth grade, my wife and I reluctantly decided to send him to another school that had a reputation of successfully motivating kids who had become turned off to school. He was resistant but we were determined since his academic skills were not improving, his behavior was worsening, and his teacher seemed either unable or unwilling to address his needs.

For the first week or so at the new school, he complained bitterly despite our belief that for the long term this was a good move. We told him that there was no other choice but to go to this school for *one semester*. At the end of the semester, we would assess the overall picture with him and decide together what would be done next. Given the magnitude of this change, we decided to establish a time frame that we thought was long enough for him to adapt to a new school but short enough to give him hope that getting back to his old school remained a possibility. It is far harder to accept *never* than *maybe*.

Within a week or two the resentment ended and by the end of the semester, he was pleased to be where he was and had absolutely no interest in returning to his old school. For most children, going to a new place or acquiring a new skill (even if it is fun at first) can be scary or frustrating. They may not realize that it often takes time to adapt to a new experience or practice to get better at any skill before they find it fulfilling. The flip side is to avoid forcing your child to continue on a path that s/he finds neither interesting nor necessary.

Teachers and coaches can often help you and your child define appropriate time or practice parameters. At school, teachers should try to identify a specific day(s) of the week that homework will (or won't) be assigned, an upper limit of time they should spend working on it and what to do if they need help. Give students a say when creating a homework calendar. As well, teachers can offer students choices within an assignment by saying, for example, "Pick any three out of the ten questions to answer. Your choice."

## REALIZE HOW VIDEO GAMES CAN BE A PLUS

Be careful about what you discourage! I have heard numerous parents and teachers complain about the amount of time their kids play video games. While virtually anything done to excess, including video games, can be problematic, a widely reported study (Chaarani et al., 2022) of nearly 2,000 children found that those who reported playing video games for three hours per day or more performed better on cognitive skills tests involving impulse control and working memory compared to children who had never played video games. Admittedly, I was shocked to learn this because it seems to defy logic and common sense with plenty of disadvantages. But the comparison was with those who had never played a video game. There is however a growing body of research that has found the benefits can sometimes dwarf the disadvantages (Zalewski, 2020).

Since video games progressively increase in degree of difficulty, most provide continuous challenges that are controlled by the player and must be mastered before moving on. Kids are motivated to keep playing because they select the level and can make it easier or more difficult depending upon how they do. That makes it possible for virtually any child to conquer the next hardest goal after a reasonable amount of practice before moving on.

Video games can therefore enhance self-esteem. Since games gradually increase in difficulty, they progressively require enhanced problem-solving skills and greater attention to detail. There are motion-controlled video games in which the player interacts with the system through body movements that can provide the equivalent of a good physical workout. Parents can find regular updates of recommended video games at all ages at pcmag.com.

## HELP YOUR CHILD DISCOVER AND PURSUE HIS/HER OWN INTERESTS

The vast majority of children will discover their various talents as they develop and become productive adults. Fulfillment occurs when *skill* meets *interest* meets *temperament*. When my daughter was in college, I strongly encouraged her to major in one of the sciences because she did very well in high school and that is where the good-paying jobs were going to be. To my dismay, she insisted upon a more liberal arts focus.

Although I was at first frustrated with her choice, I had to remind myself that it is her life and she has a right to pursue her passions rather than mine and experience whatever consequences life brings. Lead by following your child's interests. She may have had the aptitude for science but not the interest.

I think the most useful way to help our kids find their talents and interests is by encouraging them to regularly work at something that requires practice for improvement. Sports and music are so good because while few will become professionals, virtually all can get better and see their own progress through practice. Challenging kids to take the next small step in whatever the skill requires is the best way to develop inner discipline and grit. Yet it is just as important to recognize when your continuous nagging seems required for adequate motivation. If that happens, it is a good bet that the activity no longer matches your child's temperament or interest. For most children, the discovery of skill that matches interest is a long-term process that involves lots of starts and stops. One place to start is by using the "53" method (see chapter 3).

## WHEN THEY WANT TO QUIT

A dilemma often faced by multitalented children and their parents is what to do when your child pursues an interest, becomes skilled, but then wants to quit.

I was upset when my son who became a very skilled violinist told me he was no longer interested. My grandson recently quit playing baseball after having been on top teams through childhood.

Complicating matters can be pressure from a teacher or coach who may be upset at losing an accomplished performer with much "potential." When this happens, it is very important to explore your child's thoughts and feelings to provide the kind of encouragement that may be needed.

For many children, the main issue is they no longer want to devote the time and energy needed and would rather re-direct it elsewhere. In these instances, you'll just need to deal with your own disappointment at no longer going to the game or show and move on. There is nothing wrong with the child. The activity served its purpose and your child wants to pursue another of life's possibilities. They probably won't play professional basketball or earn that athletic scholarship you had hoped for. Although that can be disappointing to parents, teachers, or coaches, it is often best the for the child's well-being.

Pursuing excellence in *many* areas simultaneously can be extremely stressful and ultimately impossible. Eventually, achieving success in very competitive areas requires a very high level of commitment that may interfere with pursuing other interests or simply having time for fun and relaxation, whose importance can easily be overlooked. Often, some things have to go. By contrast, if a child wants to quit one of the very few, if not their only, ongoing activities without thought of replacement, this is more likely related to fear of failure or difficulty getting along with others. You may first want to focus your child on exploring the blockage in greater depth through a problem-solving process (chapter 8) or by reducing anxiety (see chapter 10) before making a final decision.

Teachers almost always have a few students who won't do their assignments because they fear failure. They would rather seem oppositional than feel stupid. One effective way to overcome this problem is to give at least one assignment each class that guarantees success (e.g., tell a student in advance which question you will call on her to answer, one that you are certain she knows).

## KEEP THINGS IN PERSPECTIVE

Now that I have adult children, when I look back, I realize that the vast majority of the things I found worrisome or frustrating when they were children were minor and unimportant in the grand scheme of things. Did it really matter whether my child was in the regular class or the advanced class? (One of my kids was, two weren't, and they all turned out okay.) Should I force my talented violinist son to practice? (I did, and he got really good but hated it and wound up quitting anyway.) Should I really get myself all worked up and emotional as I sit at my daughter's softball game hoping that she gets a hit, makes a play, or at least doesn't screw up? (I did, but all the worrying and hoping did not keep her from the strike-outs and errors that are part of the game.) Is it wise to have a nightly power struggle with a child who doesn't get the grades s/he is probably capable of achieving because there is a lack of interest and effort? (Many parents do, but their kids don't get better grades anyway, yet most eventually figure out life and do okay.) My kid whose room looked like a tornado is borderline obsessive about neatness as an adult. The one who feasted on burgers and fries while fighting any health food now practices yoga daily and eats veggie sandwiches on multi-grain bread.

You will minimize your aggravation and probably be much more effective dealing with these issues if you can keep things in perspective. The same goes for educators. Keep in mind that success at school requires good grades in just about everything. Honor roll at school requires a student to be highly competent in virtually all academic areas. But in the "real world" of work, competence in only one area can lead to success. And what you teach may not be "it" for every student.

Your voice is much more likely to be reassuring when a student knows their teacher understands their struggles but strongly believes in their success. This can be done by acknowledging how difficult or uninterested a student may be without attaching a negative judgment. For example, "Cameron, I know math doesn't come as easy to you as throwing a football. I totally get that you don't want to do it. Believe it or not, there may come a day when you will love to solve these kinds of math problems and be very good at it. Maybe not. Not everyone is talented at or likes the same things. I do know you will get better at this if you don't quit practicing and I also know it will be on the final exam so let's get busy getting better at this math thing."

## A closing word

At a seminar on motivation that I was conducting, a participant shared his dilemma as a father. He told me about Bill, his gifted thirteen-year-old son who did the bare minimum to pass his classes at school. The boy generally put forth little effort and got mediocre grades in most classes despite repeated discussions about the importance of doing his best interspersed with threats and actions to remove privileges as well as the promise of rewards for improvement.

I could sense that the father's relationship with his son was being dominated by the boy's poor school work ethic. Yet Bill was described as very focused and motivated when doing activities that interested him. He was also a caring, sensitive boy who often reached out in helpful ways to others who were less fortunate.

It seemed to me that there was so much positive about this boy that was getting lost in the conflict about schoolwork. I asked the father if he thought whether his son got an A or a C would matter ten or twenty years from now. After reflecting, the man said that it probably wouldn't matter, but unless he learned good study and work habits he would likely be affected in an adverse way. Further, he worried that if Bill graduated from a lesser university than he was capable of attending, his job prospects would be dim.

This father's concern is a conflict faced by many parents at various times during a child's upbringing: Do I push or back off? His eyes opened wide when I asked him if he knew people from his high school years that weren't interested or motivated in school but became successful adults and others who were "all-stars" in school but struggling in life?

Happiness and a sense of fulfillment are rarely achieved just by one's ability and effort. Also required is a good fit with one's interests and temperament. Just because I can get good at something doesn't mean I will or even should. Too much emphasis on ability without consideration for temperament can actually cripple kids emotionally.

I think about a friend's daughter, Rachel, a college graduate diagnosed as "depressed" and prescribed medication after going through weeks during which it was often a struggle for her to get out of bed.

This is a beautiful young woman with an exceptional voice who majored in music and is probably capable of a successful singing career. But she becomes filled with anxiety when performing. While applying to a prestigious music program she underwent therapy to help her quell the anxiety triggered by her upcoming audition. Although she was accepted, she never felt comfortable and eventually dropped out. After other "false starts" spanning several years, she became a music therapist and is happily employed working with children.

Parents and educators can at best guide, encourage, and provide opportunities, but at the end of the day every child must find his/her own way, and most will if we let them.

## QUESTIONS FOR REFLECTION

1. Our style of parenting is very much influenced by the parents we had or have. What did your parents do that either helped or hindered your upbringing?

2. What have you learned from this chapter that can help you highlight your child's effort even if the outcome did not meet your true standard of success?

3. What is something you'd like to improve as a parent or teacher? See if you can make this into a S.M.A.R.T. goal (e.g., I'd like to spend at least one hour alone with each child every week for the next month doing something special.) If you can't think of something specific, ask your child what s/he might like to do.

4. After identifying the S.M.A.R.T. goal, how do you plan to make it happen (e.g., Daryl and I will shoot hoops or go to the batting cage each Saturday for the next month.)?

5. Are there any ongoing issues with your child that you find frustrating? How do you react? How important do you think this issue will be when your child is an adult and you are old?

## CHAPTER 5

# How to Promote Responsibility

*When you get what you want in your struggle for self*
*And the world makes you special for a day*
*Just go to the mirror and look at yourself*
*And see what that person has to say.*

*For it isn't your parents, friends, family or class*
*Whose judgment upon you must pass*
*The someone whose verdict counts most in your life*
*Is the one looking back from the glass.*

*Some people may think you worthy of trust*
*And believe you would never lie*
*But the one in the glass says your life is a bust*
*If you can't look him straight in the eye.*

*There's the one to please, never mind all the rest*
*This someone is with you clear up to the end*
*And you've passed your most dangerous, difficult test*
*If the one in the glass is your friend.*

*You may fool the whole world on the pathway of life*
*And get pats on your back as you pass*
*But your final reward will be heartaches and tears*
*If you have cheated the one in the glass.*

CHAPTER 5

Originally "The Man in the Glass" —Anonymous

Revised by Jim Kuhnsman

A few weeks after sending our oldest son off to college a thousand miles from home, my wife and I were out to dinner feeling sentimental. As she and I talked, reality struck: we no longer had any idea about how he was living his life on a day-to-day basis. We did not know his new friends, where he went, or what he did. We knew only what he chose to tell us in our brief phone conversations. And had we wanted or needed information about his educational or health status, the university would have required his signed permission despite the fact that we were paying for every penny of his lifestyle.

Dictionary.com defines responsibility as "the opportunity or ability to act independently and make decisions without authorization. It is the "state or fact of being responsible, answerable or accountable for something within one's power, control, or management."

During a child's upbringing, parents are essential to virtually every aspect of their life, and for a good portion of each day for several years, so are educators. Yet like it or not, the eventual goal of a "successful" parent or educator is to become unnecessary! Ultimately, if we are lucky, our children will *want* to be around us but they won't *need* to be. It may be nice if we have the means to help them but not a requirement.

Barring tragedy, we must all face the day when there is no longer a shred of control we have over the whereabouts and actions of our kids. They are on their own. For responsibility to develop, getting to this day is about teaching our children to do the right thing without somebody having to look over their shoulder. It is about guiding our kids to make choices, own them, experience their benefits or consequences, and do their best to fix a bad choice and learn to make a better one.

Kids learn responsibility when we give them measured opportunities to make choices by anticipating and experiencing the consequences of the choices they make. Responsibility is a *skill* that needs to be seen, learned, practiced, and experienced. If parents and teachers make all of their child's decisions when they are young, it can be hard for them to stop and children to start when they get older.

A *New York Times* poll that looked at a nationally representative group of parents of adult children ages 18–28 found 76 percent had to remind their adult children of deadlines they needed to meet, including for schoolwork. Seventy-four percent made appointments for them, including doctor's appointments. Astoundingly, 14 percent told them which career to pursue (Quealy & Miller, 2019). These numbers may be even more pronounced given the very close proximity between many parents and their children during the pandemic that may have disrupted responsibility from its healthy development.

The skill of responsibility develops through four main building blocks. These are:

- Awareness
- Predicting
- Choosing
- Planning

Let's look at what these building blocks mean and how parents and educators can best assist their development.

## AWARENESS STRATEGIES

Awareness means paying attention to the perceptions, thoughts, feelings, and/or actions of yourself and others within a specific situation. It is cultivated by noticing what is going on around you and learning that different situations may call for different responses. Identifying a location and paying attention to where we put our phone, keys, wallet, backpack, homework, and other belongings in order to easily find them is a simple example of the importance of awareness. Missing phone calls or text messages is a consequence of misplacing our phone. Responsibility is learned when we decide to keep the phone in a specific place. As most of us know, it may take several misplacements for kids (and adults) to heighten their awareness and make a better decision.

In order to stop tapping a pencil on a desk, a child needs to first realize that he is tapping it and be aware of the distracting impact it can have on others. Awareness is about learning what to do and paying attention to doing it. The two best ways to build or improve your child's awareness are: *Explain things as you are doing them.* With a young child, explain a procedure while doing something. For example,

> Daddy and Jack are going to cross the street when the light is green. When it turns green, Dad says, "We will look both ways just to make sure there are no cars coming because cars are much bigger than people and we don't want to get hurt." It will usually take several trials before Jack automatically looks before he crosses. Until then, Dad continues to hold Jack's hand when crossing and gives feedback ("Great job, Jack. You looked before we crossed," or "Oops, Jack, I noticed you didn't look. What can happen if we don't look?").

A teacher builds awareness when s/he tells or shows students how to enter the classroom, pass in papers, or perform a host of other routines and follows through by having students practice each. I recently observed a group of middle school students behaving very well in one class after seeing the same group virtually out of control in every other class. When I asked for this teacher's special recipe, he shared how he did little else but practice appropriate behavior during the first two weeks of school!

Teaching and practice are the two main processes used to develop awareness. As children get older, sharing your experiences, especially when sensitive or hard-to-discuss matters emerge, can heighten awareness. For example, "I remember when I was younger I sometimes felt overwhelmed trying to do my best at all the activities I was involved with. I realized that I had to give some things up, but I had a really hard time deciding. Do you sometimes feel that way?"

*Notice, and then appreciate.* When your child seems to be acting without thinking or did something inappropriate, first check to make sure s/he is aware of what s/he's doing. Ask a simple question: "What are you doing?"

Follow up with, "What are you supposed to be doing?" If you get, "I don't know" to both of these questions, ask, "If you did know, what would you say?" If no response, point out the behavior ("You were interrupting while I was talking to Emily. So what are you supposed to do when you see me talking to someone?"). You may sometimes have to share the same information more than once depending on the extent of a child's age and attention span. ("Unless it's an emergency, I'll listen after I finish my conversation. When will I listen? . . . Until I finish with Emily, please think about how you can wait patiently. Thanks for waiting."). Finally, be sure to notice success and express appreciation the next few times the child did not interrupt ("You did a great job waiting. How did you make that happen?").

**Suggestion:** To help build awareness and re-direct a child, asking two simple questions is often sufficient:

- *What are you doing?*
- *What are you supposed to be doing?*

Some children can benefit from the temporary use of *props*, *cues*, or *charts* as reminders. For example, a Post-it Note on a bookbag can serve as a reminder of the items needed for school. A sticker chart for an impulsive child who has trouble waiting can help remind the child to wait for her turn. A mouse pad or carpet square for tapping a pencil at school can serve as a prop that reminds a child about not making noise. A "STOP" sign on a closed door can offer a good reminder to not barge in. One free complaint per meal, or one permitted grumble about putting the dishes away can serve as a useful tool of awareness that can reduce reminding, nagging, or arguing. Awareness leads to improved responsibility as kids get better at reminding themselves.

## PREDICTING STRATEGIES

Although there are times in life when "stuff happens" to all of us over which we have no control, children need to learn that most of their choices bring predictable results. For example, asking politely, smiling and saying "good morning" is more apt to get others to cooperate than being bossy, snarly, and withdrawn. There are three primary ways to teach kids how the things that happen to them are often predictable from their actions: *Act in a predictable way.* If you say you will do something, do it. Although life requires flexibility, keep your promises and keep things relatively on schedule. When something happens that makes it difficult or impossible to follow through on doing what you said or runs counter to what you are trying to teach, offer an explanation that makes sense. For example,

> "Bobby, I lost my temper with you today and said some things that weren't right. I feel badly about that and even worse, I've been telling you that you need to stop and think before you act. I didn't do a very good job showing you how to do that today, and like you, I need to work harder at doing the very same thing that I am trying to teach you to do."

If you can, show a preferred solution or explain why doing what you did was an appropriate exception.

*As best you can, make your environment predictable.* Children thrive when there is a predictable time and place. For example, if possible, set aside a place for your child to do his homework. Identify a time for laundry to get folded. Help her figure out where to put her completed assignments, hang her coat, and keep her pencils. Have a specific place in the garage for her bike. Ideally, involve your child in making these decisions.

*Encourage predicting by asking questions.* Ask questions that help kids anticipate what is likely to happen when they make certain choices. For example:

a. Most teachers like things turned in on time. What do you think Mrs. Cary might say or do if you turn in the assignment late?

b. You complain that I nag you a lot and that I'm a neat freak. How do you think I might react if you straightened your room without being told?

c. What do you think might happen to your playing time if you skip practice today?

d. It sounds like Juanita has been picking on you. What do you think she would do if you walked away? Agreed with everything she said? Hit her? Told your teacher? Had me call your teacher?

e. I know your sister can really be a pain when your friends come over. What do you think would happen if you invited her to be with you and your friends for a few minutes and then told her that since they were your friends you want to spend some time with them alone? If she became annoying when you asked, how do you think things would go if you gave her a choice to either leave on her own or involve me?

f. Jalen, what am I likely to say or do if you ask me to drive you to your friend's house before you take out the garbage that's still sitting there?

## CHOOSING STRATEGIES

All kids are faced with daily mundane decisions such as how much time to devote to schoolwork, who to hang out with, which television show to watch, what to wear, and what to eat. At some point in their lives, most young people feel pressured to do things that parents and teachers may dread even thinking about: skipping school, drinking or taking drugs, having sex, joining a gang, etc. The best way to prepare your child to make good choices is to start giving them opportunities early and often. I recall working with a mom who couldn't get her three-year-old to put on his coat. She solved this problem by giving him a simple choice, suggesting: "Put your favorite sleeve on first." To her surprise, he reached out with one of his arms. Another strategy is to categorize activities as "have to" (e.g., homework, dog walking, setting the table, going to church) or "want to" (e.g., listen to music, play video games, talk to friends, watch a favorite TV show). Most kids (and adults) find it easier to handle "drudgery" when they can look forward to a preferred activity shortly after.

**Suggestion**: Look for opportunities every day to offer choices. For the most part, does it really matter what they eat, what they wear, or the music they prefer? Start by offering simple choices. At very early ages, toddlers can decide which toy to play with or what to eat (from among limited options). As kids get older, choices can be more open-ended. For example, "Mary, when did you say you were taking the dog for a walk?" Keep in mind that too much choice can be overwhelming but too few fails to teach the child how to think and make decisions. Below are more examples of choice. You can begin or end each with "Which works better for you?":

- Go to the store with me or stay here with your sister.
- Clean up your mess now or after dinner.
- Do the laundry or wash the dishes.
- When you are angry, tell how you feel, take a few deep breaths, write a note, or go to your room until you calm down.
- Peanut butter and jelly or grilled cheese for lunch?
- Pick any shirt with long sleeves. You choose.
- Forget to come home on time and give up using the car for a week or remember and keep the privilege.

## PLANNING STRATEGIES

A goal without a plan is a dream. We all have hopes and dreams but to be realized, a plan is necessary. Regular planning is especially appropriate for kids who are impulsive, have trouble organizing, become overwhelmed easily, or do not anticipate consequences of their actions. For a plan to be successful it must:

1. *Be specific:* Ask: "What do you want to have happen?"

- I want to get the latest video game.
- I want to get a better grade on the next test.
- I want to stay calm and think about what to do if someone does something I don't like.
- I want to be a professional basketball player.

*2. Identify action(s) to take:* Ask: "How do you plan to make it happen?"

- To earn money, I'll let Ms. Jones and Ms. Ray know that I can babysit.
- I'll study at least fifteen minutes more each day and go to the "review" class before the next test.
- If I get angry at someone, I'll take a few deep breaths and think about possible consequences before I act.
- I'll practice three-point shots for at least a half hour every day.

*3. Include ways to handle obstacles that might occur:* Ask: "That sounds like a good idea but just in case (something happens that gets in the way):

- Ms. Jones and/or Ms. Ray don't ask you to babysit, what other things might you do to earn some money?
- Your friends text or call while you are studying or you get invited to do something that is more fun, how will you finish what you started?
- If taking a few deep breaths doesn't calm you, what else can you do to settle down?
- You might have to miss the game. How will you handle that?

**Suggestion:** Planning is one of the best strategies to use when a child breaks rules either at home or somewhere else. It is probably the most time-consuming and most likely to lead to long-term change. Since long-term change rarely happens right away, it is almost always necessary to use the process more than once. Lead your child through the following planning process. Notice the purpose of each step:

- What did you do that got you into trouble? (*the problem*)
- When you did that, what did you think would happen? (*think before you act*)
- What else could you have done (aim for the child to list at least two other possibilities that would be acceptable)? (*how could the problem have been better solved?*)
- What will you do the next time you are faced with a similar situation? (*choose-predict-plan*)
- In case you do this again, what do you think should happen? (*anticipate consequences before you act*)
- Explore additional consequences if you think they will teach or reinforce better behavior.

Having a clear plan makes achieving even very difficult goals more likely. For example, only a very select few who want to become a professional athlete, musician or astrophysicist will, but without practice there is no chance! To encourage improved behavior, leading a child through a planning meeting can be a good consequence in and of itself.

## MORE STRATEGIES TO PROMOTE RESPONSIBILITY

*Give opportunities to make regular family and/or community contributions.* Children who have regular responsibilities (call these "contributions") develop a feeling of healthy achievement and a sense of community: I'm part of something more than just me. I have the power to impact others.

**Suggestion:** Make a list of all the things that have to get done each day in order for the family to properly function. Examples might include vacuuming, walking or feeding the dog, doing laundry, cleaning, putting out the recyclables, preparing a meal, and assisting a family member with doing something that person is not yet able to do. They can be involved in deciding and any that nobody chooses can be decided on by drawing straws or in some other way taking turns. As a teacher, you might use the list of classroom responsibilities (fig. 1) as a starter.

Within the community/school, how can your child help make it a better place? Religious and community non-profit agencies often provide opportunities. A few churches and synagogues in my community provide temporary housing for a homeless family every month for one week. Several member families including children of all ages contribute their time and energy providing necessities like setting up sleeping arrangements, hosting, cooking, cleaning, and transporting. Kids from the congregations often play or hang out with children in residence.

### Responsible Jobs in the Classroom (Figure 1.)

Class Greeter
Absentee Caller
Errand Runner
Paper Distributor
Assignment Collector
Area Quieter
Materials Supplier
Office Reporter
Work Hanger
Dispute Mediator
Cheerer Upper

*Expect caring, sensitive behavior from your child.* It is never too early or late to begin teaching children how to show caring, respect, and sensitivity toward other people. Rude behavior should be dealt with in a caring but firm way as soon as it occurs without attacking a child's dignity. A simple, "That was rude!" or "We don't do (say) that!" given firmly should be followed by discussing why the behavior was hurtful and then teaching a better alternative: "When we don't like someone we can walk away from them or try to find something about them we can like," or "Can you think of some ways to help Mary be nicer without yelling and saying mean things to her?" If no response, offer a possibility or two and then have your child practice.

**Suggestion:** The growing attention to eliminating entrenched forms of systemic racism and other hateful "isms," gives us opportunities to sensitize our child to the problems certain words and actions can cause. Kids need to know that all forms of bullying are about people trying to feel powerful at the expense of others. It can help to ask questions like:

- *Has there ever been a time when somebody treated you unfairly (was mean for no reason)?*
- *How did that feel?*
- *Did anyone stand up for or help you?*
- *How would you have helped if a friend of yours was in a similar situation?*

If you learn that your child is being a bully, you need to help her know how to gain more positive attention but at the same time firmly deal with the harmful behavior. For example, "It is not now or ever okay to verbally attack or pick on someone else. Calling Carly gay and sending hurtful stuff on the internet is totally unacceptable. You are better than that. How are you going to make things right?"

These days it can also help by looking inside to explore how we may be talking about people in our lives who see things in ways that are different from us. In the privacy of our homes, we may sometimes loudly vent our negative feelings about a co-worker or politician at the dinner table without realizing that using harsh language, hate, or aggressive actions to air grievances can make it seem okay for our children to act out in hurtful ways.

If reports of bullying persist, there are likely more deep-seated emotional issues that need to be explored with a mental health professional.

*Respectfully stand up for what is right.* Several years ago, when my oldest son was in middle school, he was chosen to be in the National Junior Honor Society. Selection was based on grades and teacher recommendations. A school assembly with students and parents of those selected would be held to honor selectees and my son was asked to be a main speaker. He is not shy, so to my wife's and my surprise, he neither wanted to attend the ceremony nor speak.

After asking him to explain, he proceeded to tell us that he thought the process of selection was unfair. As an example, he talked about a peer who he strongly felt should have been selected but wasn't and how upset that child was. Like most parents, I was very proud of his achievement and wanted to bask in the glow of his success. But he held his ground, arguing that he wanted no part of a process that honored certain students at the expense of others. Although I felt a bit disappointed, I could not have been more proud of him holding firm to his beliefs that focused not just on what was good for him but for others as well.

**Suggestion:** As discussed earlier, responsibility is about doing the right thing, not because you are told to do it, but because it is the right thing to do.

It is so important to picture ourselves at the receiving end of our behaviors before we act. The best way to teach empathy is to be guided by how you would feel if somebody did to you what you are about to do to get your way. Avoid doing anything that you would consider dangerous, damaging, or disrespectful (the 3 D's) if done to you. Kids take notice and are likely to be influenced by the behavior of those they admire.

*Take other people's feedback seriously.* It is not unusual for parents to want to defend and side with their children when others outside the family express concerns about behavior.

When our kids get into trouble, we might want to believe that it must be the fault of the strict teacher, the bad influence of another child or a stage that will be outgrown. Perhaps it is. However, as tough as it is to hear negatives about our child, we should listen carefully.

It is far more common to hear complaints from parents about their own children than it is about others. Most children will behave better outside the home than they do at home, so hearing concerns from others is a red flag that warrants deeper exploration. If you become upset, calm yourself down, and then later share the feedback with your child. This can help you understand why there is a problem and make you better able to lead to some helpful solutions.

**Suggestion:** It is upsetting to hear unpleasant news about our child from others. As hard as it may be, try to stay calm and ask questions to get as much information as you can. Avoid defending or explaining the behavior unless you know the cause and it is not a pattern. Express appreciation to the person for alerting you and then explore with your child. For example, *"Evan, Mrs. Jones called with some upsetting news that has to do with Billy on the school bus. Do you have any idea what she might have said?"* If *"no"* or silence ensues, after a pause let him know: *"She told me that Billy is getting badly teased on the bus and thinks you are involved. What's going on?"* If there is denial or rationalization (e.g., *"It wasn't me; there were lots of kids."*), explore further (e.g., *"So it wasn't just you. There are other kids involved as well. Why do you think Mrs. Jones is very concerned that her son is being teased and bullied? How do you think he feels?"*)

If your child acknowledges responsibility, be sure to appreciate honesty but express disappointment ("I'm glad you are accepting responsibility, but what you did is obviously not right and very disappointing. I expect better from you."). Discussion may follow, but conclude by seeking a solution (e.g., "What are you going to do to make things right?").

If the solution seems inappropriate or incomplete, you may need to teach your child a better way. For example, "I think you owe him an apology and a promise not to do that again. If he were here right now, how would you say that?" Conclude with a plan going forward (e.g., "How will you help put an end to this?").

Parents and teachers may find one or more of the questions in figure 2 helpful when teaching responsibility.

### Responsibility Questions (Figure 2.)

What happened?
What were you trying to do? Did it work?
What was wrong with what you did?
How can you help rather than hurt?
How can you fix the problem?

If something like this happens again, what will you do differently?

What consequence(s) should there be for what you did?

If this happens again, what do you think should happen to you or to others who stood by and did nothing?

## Questions for Reflection

1. Make a list of things you do for your kids every day. How many of these things could they do for themselves? What might happen if you let them do more of those things?

2. Do you ever find yourself scolding, yelling, or nagging about the same issue? What is the issue? Why is it important that your child do it your way? What else might you do to promote responsibility?

3. One of the ways children learn to be responsible is by helping others. What are some possibilities for your child?

4. If your child is "forgetful" or "impulsive," what questions, props, or choices might you use to help her become more aware?

5. How is a promise different from a plan?

# CHAPTER 6

# Limits, Rewards, and Consequences

*When parents say "because I said so," you know you made a good argument.*

—HOLLYWOODLIFE.COM

FRIENDS OF MINE WHO HAVE A NINETEEN-YEAR-OLD SON WITH NO JOB recently shared that he and his not quite eighteen-year-old girlfriend were about to move in together. When I asked how they were going to support themselves, my friends planned to give them money each month from what they had set aside for his college education. Since his girlfriend's parents were very strict, they were not going to provide resources to their unmarried teenage daughter who had no means of independent financial support.

My friends scoffed at that decision. They made it sound like this poor girl and her boyfriend had to endure a set of uncool parents trying to block their way. While I love my friends, this was merely their latest response in a lifetime of enabling a young man accustomed to getting whatever he wants. From my perspective, her parents were simply trying to protect her from an ill-advised charade that had little chance of ending well.

As parents and educators, we should feel badly and apologize when we attack a child's dignity, not when we block the seductive doorway of momentary pleasure that masks danger and pain. Despite a plethora of messages that impact our children from peers and media, they are most influenced by their parents and some of their teachers. As parents and educators, we need to establish predictable limits based on solid values to give our kids a firm foundation.

Rarely does it end well when parents are afraid to set limits or feel guilty and judge themselves as mean when they do. I have seen some loving parents knowingly teach their kids the wrong values probably out of guilt or springing from their own insecurity to be loved; buying a nagging teenage girl a halter top see-through blouse; allowing a booze party at the house because "they're going to drink anyway"; getting an expensive toy because everyone else supposedly has it.

I have seen some parents look the other way when a child calls them an "idiot" or talks to their teacher disrespectfully. Some threaten the school if their child gets a poor grade instead of focusing on what their child should do differently to get a better result. While many school administrators at least publicly back their teachers while providing corrective feedback, privately, when necessary, some take the side of the complaining parent(s), which fails to teach a child how to avoid or better manage conflict.

Setting limits for our children requires us to model in our lives what we want them to do in theirs. That means being aware of how we talk to or about other people and how we act toward them and our environment. The old proverbial adage reminds us that the apple rarely falls far from the tree. If we want our child not to nag us (most kids will on average ask nine times for what they want before most parents cave), we need to not nag them. If we yell at our kids, then it is fair to expect that they will yell back at us or at their siblings or classmates when they don't get their way. If we hit them to show what is right from wrong, expect them to hit others when they think they are right and others are wrong.

Try to act in ways that you want your children to be even if it may not feel comfortable for a while. For example, if you tend to quickly lose your temper and say nasty things you might later regret, try to stay silent and walk away until you can address the issue rationally. If you want your child to value the importance of doing well at school, make sure she sees you reading a book at least half as often as you watch TV. Success in life is most likely when parents set clear limits around putting forth effort at school, helping at home, practicing a skill until mastery is gained, and acting respectfully at all times including when you disagree with somebody.

## Time-in saves time-out

Understand that misbehavior is often fueled by a developmental need or as an expression of a child seeking fulfillment of one or more of her needs. For example, a two-year-old and a teenager are oppositional because those are stages of life where there is a developmental need to practice independence. By contrast, a change in life circumstances such as the arrival of a new baby, bickering between parents, or a move to a new school may create a feeling of insecurity and more attention-seeking behavior.

My sense is that each child has an "internal need thermostat," and if they don't get enough of what their thermostat tells them they need, then they become more likely to do irritating things or self-destructive things that force others to take notice. For example, the father of Kristin, a bright four-year-old girl and a new baby, was exasperated with her willful behavior. He claimed that she was doing things like soiling her pants despite fully knowing better and taking juice and pouring it on the floor right in front of him or his wife. Things were getting worse despite either rewards for good behavior or time-out for bad.

I suggested that this caring father spend at least as much time doing an enjoyable activity with her (attention) as the time being spent trying to get her to clean up the spill or use the toilet. I further suggested that during this enjoyable time, he ask her for help in solving *his problem* (e.g., "Daddy has a problem and maybe you can help, Kristin. Would you like to help?" When you need to poop and you do it in your pants, it takes so much time for me to clean and change you. I am so tired from working that I get even more tired. Can you help me?").

Although a bit uncertain at first, to his amazement, Kristin had all kinds of ideas about what she could do to "help," which quickly helped turn things around.

Since Kristin's "thermostat" was registering greater needs for attention and control, likely due to the presence of the baby, by giving her attention before an incident and using some of that time together to "empower" her as a helper, they were able to get past these issues pretty quickly.

## No cost rewards

Before we explore how to most effectively use traditional rewards, don't miss the many opportunities that undoubtedly occur every day to "catch your child being good." We often fail to notice when things are going smoothly or we notice but stay silent.

Be generous in sharing your appreciations because they are the best way to reinforce the values you want your child to acquire. We sometimes forget how important our feedback is in determining how our kids think, feel, and act. It is easy to notice when we are interrupted by our child during a conversation with a friend, but it takes effort to notice when we are not. We hardly notice when our car starts, but it sure gets a lot of our attention when it does not.

Regularly make the effort to notice when things are going well. For example, "I like the way you waited and occupied yourself while I was talking on the phone. Thanks for being patient," or, "I am so impressed to see you reading without being reminded." In addition, rewarding with things or extra privileges or trying to find an effective consequence is rarely necessary when we:

- *Show excitement in our child's discoveries:* I love how excited you get when I see (hear) you_____.

- *Acknowledge their insights in a conversation:* I hadn't thought of that; What a cool idea!; You make a great point.

- *Notice an act of self-sacrifice:* Sharing your candy was really thoughtful; I hope you feel proud volunteering to serve hungry people. I sure am.

- *Ask for an opinion:* What do you think we should do about_____?

- *Listen to their experiences and stories*

**Suggestion:** Appreciate and encourage at least as often or more than correct. In his book *They Call Me Coach*, John Wooden, the legendary basketball coach during UCLA's magical years of winning ten national college basketball championships in twelve years, including seven in a row offered the following advice:

> "End practice on a happy note." I wanted the boys to want to come out to practice, and I wanted them to get a certain amount of pleasure out of basketball. It's a game. It should be fun. So I always tried to counterbalance any criticism in practice with a bit of praise. I wanted my players to feel that the worst punishment I could give them was to deny them the privilege of practicing. If they did not want to practice, I did not want them there.

As the saying goes, "You can attract more bees with honey than with vinegar." Make a habit of liberally using these fifteen positive comments especially after you notice a child's improvement:

1. Way to go!

2. How thoughtful you were when you_____.

3. Wow—that was outstanding!

4. That was awesome.

5. You really hung in there.

6. Your effort has really brightened my day. Thanks.

7. Look at the smile you have put on my face.

8. I hope you feel proud, because you should.

9. That was quite an accomplishment.

10. Congratulations.

11. I was so impressed today when_____.

12. This was tough but you had the patience to figure it out. Keep it up.

13. I am one lucky parent (teacher) to have a child like you.

14. The progress I saw today was impressive.

15. That took a special effort.

## WHEN AND HOW TO USE TRADITIONAL REWARDS

Rewards are objects, privileges, and special events. They can be used effectively within narrow guidelines to reinforce appropriate behavior. They may have a regular place if you have a very difficult child or special needs child with behavioral or cognitive limitations. For example, Molly often hits when she is frustrated. She has limited language skills. While teaching her a non-aggressive word or sign to express frustration, her teacher decides to give her a sticker every half hour when she uses the word/sign and/or doesn't hit. When she earns a certain number of stickers, she gets a special object or certain privilege. Ultimately, the goal is for her to not hit without needing a pay off, and little by little the time interval required to earn the reward becomes longer and longer until the skill is acquired. It is then discontinued.

For most kids, we can inadvertently turn a reward that motivates into a "bribe" that spoils. Notice how easily that can happen: "If you do your homework every day this week, you can earn a trip to the amusement park this weekend." This type of trade-off is rarely effective in the long run because kids come to expect some type of external payoff for doing the right thing and they up the ante. One week it may be a trip to the amusement park while the next it may be an unhealthy dose of junk food or a new video game. Parents and teachers can start feeling like they are being held hostage. I recall a situation at one of my schools where a sixth-grade child had been promised a trip to Australia if he showed improvement in his grades.

A truly effective reward is not something promised but instead given only *occasionally* and *unexpectedly* and only *after* an accomplishment as an expression of appreciation. Notice the difference between a reward and a bribe.

*Bribe:* When you get your homework done, we'll go out for ice cream.

*Reward:* You seemed to work hard getting your homework done. Let's go out and get an ice cream!

In the first example, a reward becomes a bribe by making it a promise. Going out for ice cream is promised *if and when* homework is done. It creates an expectation that a reward should follow for doing the right thing. While we want kids to value a *When–Then* connection (accomplishing a "have to" before doing a "want to"), we don't want them dependent on a reward for doing what is expected. In the second example, it is an expression of appreciation for an accomplishment and is given only occasionally and unexpectedly.

If child asks for a reward, be non-committal. For example, Michael asks, "Can we get ice cream if I get my homework done?" The best answer is, "Ask me again after it's done." And when you are asked again, be sure to say something like, "We can go today or another day this week. You choose."

**Suggestion:** If you have more than one child, it can be very effective to reward the family on behalf of an individual's accomplishment. Sibling rivalry is minimized in families when parents allow all children to benefit from each other's victories. For example, at a dinner with everyone present, Mom might say, "Congratulations, Elijah, on your really nice progress report. To celebrate, let's all head out for an ice cream after dinner." A teacher might say to her class, "We won't have time to celebrate things every day, but in honor of Zach's cooperation today, all of us get an extra period of recess."

## SAY WHAT YOU WANT CALMLY, FIRMLY, AND RESPECTFULLY

Much of the time, the best way to set limits is to clearly express your own thoughts and feelings in an assertive way. Use "I" messages. For example, "I feel very strongly about this issue, Lily. You think you should stay out as late as you want, and while I agree that you usually make good decisions, rarely if ever does anything good happen beyond the time of your curfew, and I don't want to stay awake worrying."

Depending upon age and maturity, stay open to modifying your position if you hear a solution from your child that you can live with as well or nearly as well. Try to stay away from a more scolding posture, such as, "When you're old enough to be living on your own and you are paying your own bills, then you can come in whenever you want!"

**Suggestion:** When you set a limit and your child complies, make sure you notice. For example:

1. "Felice, your room needs straightening."

After compliance,

"Wow, Felice, you hung up your clothes as I asked. Thanks for your help."

2. "Martha, when you think I'm being unfair, I appreciate you telling me calmly rather than with an angry tone. Please take a few deep breaths, settle down, and then tell me how you feel."

After a few moments of compliance,

"Before we continue, do you notice that we have been talking calmly and respectfully even though we still don't see things the same way? I appreciate that. Let's keep going and see if we can figure something out that can work for both of us."

3. "Denise, you can't punch your brother even if he is being annoying. You can either ignore him and stay here or go to your room and close your door."

After compliance,

"You went to your room when your brother was bothering you. I appreciate that. How did that work out for you?"

When seeking compliance from headstrong children, it may be necessary to hit the repeat button more than once. Be a "broken record." If something is important to you, be prepared to persist. Fight the temptation to give up easily. Let your child know what s/he did, how you feel, and what you want. For example, "I feel_____when you_____. Next time_____, I want/expect_____." It can be easy to cave in with tough kids because of the emotional exhaustion their behavior creates.

## USE CONSEQUENCES EFFECTIVELY

Beginning early, children need specific instruction on how to behave in various situations (sometimes several times) along with firm reminders and consequences when they cross the line. Otherwise, the delightfully indulged younger child will turn into a spoiled adolescent and narcissistic adult.

We need to intervene the first time a child bites, refuses to share, pulls hair, pinches, throws food, hits another child, or swears. For example, the child needs to hear our displeasure in a calm yet firm no-nonsense manner, asked what else s/he could have done in that situation, and if necessary, shown a better, less harmful alternative. It may be necessary to warn your child of a privilege to be removed if the behavior continues, although don't promise a consequence you know you won't deliver (e.g., "If you do that again, no TV for a month!").

A good consequence should teach better behavior, and the best way to do that is to relate the consequence to a behavior as directly as possible, so the child sees, feels, and experiences the results of his actions. It is important to avoid techniques that attack dignity such as physical punishment, blame, verbal abuse, and the withholding of love since these techniques succeed only in making kids feel stupid, dumb, afraid, or angry.

The idea is to connect the consequence to the action whenever possible. Missing a meal, eating leftovers, or preparing your own meal are examples of a *natural* consequence for coming home after dinner is served. Cleaning a mess is a *logical* consequence of making a mess. Doing a good deed that gives back something helpful to someone is a *logical* consequence of having said or done something hurtful. Losing use of the car for a specified amount of time is a *logical* consequence of driving recklessly, coming home late, creating unnecessary worry, or avoiding the fulfillment of home/school responsibilities.

**Suggestion:** Consequences have to be tailored to the child since what might be effective for one may not be for another. For example, a stern sharing of your worry about safety with a child who breaks curfew may be sufficient for a child with good impulse control but inadequate for another who tends to act first and think later.

Time-out can be an effective consequence when used infrequently and for the purposes of reflection and/or planning. For example, "Take a time-out and come back when you are ready to apologize for hitting your brother and can say what else you can do besides hitting when you are mad."

If an inappropriate behavior persists, the child is usually seeking relief from frustration or lacks a more appropriate way to express their needs. The best solution is to identify and address its cause(s). Consequences may be a *small part* of a solution to continued inappropriate behavior, but it is *not the* solution. As noted before, identifying the likely cause(s) of the behavior(s) and addressing it/them may require professional intervention. Do not shy away from seeking help!

In most instances, establishing effective limits takes persistence and can wear you down, but it is really not that difficult, especially when the message rarely varies and it is begun early. You want to teach proper behavior, stop unacceptable behavior, explain how it was harmful, and expect the child to fix things as best as possible.

For example, two-year-old Jasmine throws food on the floor. Mother makes eye contact, gets close to Jasmine, remains calm, and tells her slowly in a firm voice that food is not for throwing and needs to be picked up now. If it happens again, Mom pauses the meal and says, "All done eating. Time to help Mama clean up." If she won't, Mom avoids making a fuss and cleans up while ignoring Jasmine's misguided but developmentally normal behavior when a two-year-old wants to feel in control and may lack the words. The meal continues shortly thereafter with a reminder: "We say 'all done'; we don't throw food." If it happens again during the same meal, the child has either eaten enough or dislikes the food, and the meal ends or the menu changes if there are other options.

Naturally, there are times when having children experience the consequences of their actions would be harmful or dangerous. Obviously, a child should not have to burn her hand to learn not to touch a hot stove or receive a shock to learn not to play with electrical outlets or get beaten by a bully before learning to present oneself in a more assertive manner.

When minor but irritating behavior keeps happening, you may need get creative and think outside the box when connecting a consequence. Illustrated in the examples below are some clever and powerful ways to use *natural* and *logical* consequences in those instances. You may need to tweak or vary these examples to best fit your situation:

> *The charitable bag.* When my sons were about ten and eleven years old (they were born one year apart), I grew tired of picking up after them. I thought our expectation that all family members have a responsibility to pick up after themselves in "family community" places like the den, foyer, and living room was reasonable but it was largely ignored by them.
>
> After a number of reminders to little avail, I decided on a different approach. I was spurred on by lying down to relax on the family room couch after a tiring day at work, only to find a pair of kid-sized dirty underwear wedged and partially hidden between two cushions. Fighting the urge to throw it at them, which I had already done more than once before, a new procedure came to mind. I would put all clothes and other belongings that I saw lying around in a big lawn bag. All family members would have until Friday to look through the bag to claim objects they might want to keep. Anything left would be taken to a charity and donated. I asked my sons for suggestions about which

charities they would most want to support. Needless to say, after a few of their favorite objects were donated because they neglected to check the bag, this problem dramatically decreased.

*Wash only what is in the laundry basket.* Stop searching for dirty clothes. You put in the washer only what is in the laundry basket.

*The jungle room.* The parents of a child with a messy room refused to enter unless it was clean. They called it the jungle and told the child to keep the door to the jungle closed. They never said the child had to keep the room clean, but when the child needed a lightbulb fixed or something else done in the room, the parents explained that they wouldn't go into the jungle. When the child needed enough help, s/he cleaned the room.

*The supervised school jaunt.* When Sullivan kept missing his bus because of fussing at home, his mother made him walk. To be sure he was safe, the mother drove a few yards behind, out of eyesight, to see that he got to school safely.

*No manners, no privilege.* **After repeated reminders** to use good manners like saying "please" and "thank you" with limited success, a mom I know took ice-cream cones she had just bought her children and without saying a word, tossed them in the garbage after they failed to express gratitude and use proper manners when ordering. When they reacted with shock, she told them that perhaps next time they would remember to use proper manners when asking for and receiving something they want.

*The dead fish lesson.* Without saying a word, a mom didn't prepare a meal for her son after his pet fish died because he had neglected to feed it. When he asked for his meal, she used that moment to emphasize the importance of following through on responsibilities and promises made, especially when they impact others who depend on them. If he was hungry, he would have to prepare his own meal.

*The wheel of misfortune.* A high school teacher I know develops a wheel patterned after the game show but with consequences listed between the spokes. If a student breaks a rule, they get a choice of a consequence that she decides or they can spin the wheel. She identifies her consequence only after the student decides. The wheel includes one slot identified as "get off scot free."

## WHICH "CONSEQUENCE" WOULD BEST TEACH YOU?

It is important to realize that while children may not understand things as well as adults, they are just as likely to feel and react as we do. Put yourself at the receiving end of each of the problem situations below and decide which "consequence" would be more likely to teach you a lesson without making you feel belittled. While some of these may sound silly because you are an adult, consider that scolding, losing privileges, being in time-out, getting the silent treatment, writing a child's name on a chalkboard, and giving a writing assignment about wrongdoing are not unusual consequences in some schools and/or homes. Consider the emotional impact any of these examples may have. Keep in mind that an effective consequence should connect to the behavior and discourage a repeat without triggering a desire for payback. Which would best do that for you?

## SITUATION 1
### You are Late to the Airport

1. You miss your plane and have to pay a penalty to change your ticket.

2. You are told to go into the baggage room and write a hundred times, "I won't be late to the airport again."

## SITUATION 2
## Your Significant other Asked You to Buy a Favored Snack Food at the Store but You Forgot

1. You apologize for your oversight and go back to the store when asked.

2. You can't find the favorite snack food, and when you ask your partner if s/he knows where it is, s/he scoldingly says, "Maybe next time I ask you to buy something for me, you won't forget!"

## SITUATION 3
## You Spill Coffee While You are Eating

1. You are scolded for being a "careless slob."

2. You are handed a sponge.

## SITUATION 4
## You Agree to Tidy Up the Bedroom as Requested Several Times by Your Significant other but You Get Preoccupied and Forget

1. S/he acts impatient, cold, and distant but doesn't say anything.

2. You find all of your stuff that wasn't put away piled onto your side of the bed.

## SITUATION 5
## You Did Not Get the Report to your Boss on Time

1. Your boss tells you the likely consequences to the company because the report isn't there and asks you how you plan to fix the problem.

2. You lose use of your office for a week.

3. Your name is publicly posted on a daily list of "poor performers" in the company newsletter.

## Be very selective before raising your voice

A raised voice to express disapproval or anger as a consequence or while giving a consequence is only effective when it is used rarely. Violent verbal or non-verbal expressions of anger usually provokes fear and shuts down the rational brain, making it virtually impossible for learning to happen. As such, since the goal is for the child to understand that what s/he did was inappropriate and why, and for the parent to understand the child's actions in order to decide how to best prevent it from happening again, it is rarely productive or effective.

At most, limit using a raised voice to times of danger or when you really want to get a point across because you consider the issue to be especially important. A raised voice should be like a double exclamation point or words in boldface lettering. Kids usually tune out adults who yell frequently, since they are unable to differentiate what is really important from what sounds like the everyday nagging they have to endure. By contrast, an unexpected raised voice, like a flashing red light sends a powerful message that says, "stop" or "enough" or at least, "pay attention."

## Dealing with lying

Most kids lie because they are afraid of trouble if they tell the truth. They worry about disapproval or punishment if they reveal what they did or own up when caught. The first step is to lower the stakes by exploring why the child felt the need to lie. For example, Dave comes home and is asked by his dad if he has any homework. Dave says no.

A few days later, Dave's teacher calls to say that Dave has not been doing his homework. Dave's father is upset that he has been lied to and is tempted to give an angry lecture coupled with a loss of privileges. However, he decides to use this as an opportunity to explore with Dave issues about school as well as honesty. He says, "Dave, your teacher called today and said that you have not been doing your homework and your grades are suffering. The other day when I asked, you said that you had no homework to do. I am concerned about that, and I'd like to hear what you have to say."

Dave uncomfortably wiggles in his chair, looks away, and says, "I don't know." His father continues, "Dave, you probably feel uncomfortable right now and maybe even worried that what you say might get you into trouble. And maybe there will be consequences. But the most important thing is that we figure out what is blocking you from doing what is required to be successful. What's going on?"

Perhaps Dave avoids the homework because he doesn't understand the material but is afraid to ask for help; maybe he has trouble organizing his priorities and puts playing video games ahead of doing homework; maybe he doesn't see the purpose of doing homework because he already knows the material and is bored by having to do a repetitive task; maybe he is doing drugs and is afraid to own up.

If Dave doesn't answer or seems unsure, Dad should offer some of these reasons or others below in third person: "You know, Dave, sometimes students don't do their homework because _____. Other times, something else is going on. Since nothing is more important to me than your well-being, help me understand why you think this is happening and what we might do about it." However the discussion ends, it is wise to monitor and follow up. This may mean checking with the teacher on the next few assignments or monitoring Dave's whereabouts a bit more carefully.

Some children tell lies as a way to make their lives seem more interesting. At our daughter's first-grade parent-teacher conference, her teacher told us how often she expressed enthusiasm about horseback riding. Earlier, we had received a phone call from the same teacher expressing concern about the impact our marital breakup seemed to be having on our child. The only problem was that our daughter had never been horseback riding and our marriage was solid. Confronting her with these events, she seemed uncomfortable. Our strategy was to praise her as a wonderful "story-teller" and teach her that the best storytellers can tell great "pretend" stories, but it could be scary and embarrassing to tell a story when other people think what you are saying is real. The "lying" stopped.

Sometimes kids are angry with a sibling, teacher, parent, or student and they may make false negative claims against them to get even. These children need to learn how to directly express their hurts and wants. With younger kids, teach and practice the "bug/want" strategy. "It *bugs* me when_____. I *want* you to_____." With older kids, the "three-step express" as an "I" message is an alternative:

1. When (say what the other person did)

2. I feel (say how you feel)

3. I want (say what you want to happen)

Sometimes there is no direct evidence that a child is lying, but you have strong suspicions. When that happens, you can say, "I get the feeling that I am not hearing the whole story. Tell me more about_____."

Finally, there is "fun lying" that may even become part of our culture as in the tooth fairy and Santa Claus. One way to deal with it is to up the ante by playing along and increasing the story line.

*Child:* "Yesterday I climbed a mountain three times. It was great."

*Adult:* "I once climbed two mountains, walked through the desert, and then flew to China in one day. It was great, too. Do you think I really did all of that in one day or am I making up a story and having fun with you?" This changes a lie into a fun game and removes the reason for the lie by making it ineffective as a way to fool you.

**Suggestion:** To minimize lying, it is important that we regularly let our kids know that we understand their desires and conflicts or want to. For example, "I don't expect you to always tell me everything you do, but there are two important things I want you to know. "First, I don't ever want you to put yourself in a dangerous situation, but if you are ever in one (for example, other kids are drinking and you need to get home), call or tell me. Your safety is more important to me than any mistake you could ever possibly make. Second, don't lie. If I ask about something, either tell what happened or just say, "I'd rather not talk about it right now."

## THE LIMITATION OF CONSEQUENCES

Of course, real life is not always as simple as the examples above, and there is no foolproof substitute for using good common sense. Further, there are no simple consequences to fix chronic problems of defiance such as refusal to do schoolwork, harmful aggression directed toward self or others, and impulsive acting-out.

Some schools and parents believe it is "fair" to use the same consequences for all kids without regard to whether or not they get the desired result. A better definition of "fair" is to do your best to give each child what s/he needs. For example, earning a zero for not doing a school assignment can be a very effective reminder for students who are achievement oriented and rarely, if ever, get poor grades. By contrast, a student who has repeatedly gotten zeroes is highly unlikely to improve if s/he gets another. Since some students who have stopped putting forth effort fear failure, change will only occur if their teacher makes it hard for them to fail. They need *more success experiences* and *fewer consequences* to move from "I can't" to "I can."

My granddaughter (Meg) in middle school could not find her homemade lunch one day. It was nowhere to be found. She has a severe case of celiac disease and must be extremely careful about her diet to avoid severe headaches often lasting days. To solve the mystery, a school camera had captured another child stealing her lunch. Both my granddaughter and the child who took her lunch were called to the office. The other girl acknowledged taking her lunch. When looked into more deeply, it was discovered that this child was barely getting enough to eat in her impoverished home. Had Meg known, I am quite certain she would have offered to share or outright given her the lunch, but as we know, many kids would be too embarrassed to say something. The incident ended with Meg and the other child donating their time to help at the local food cupboard with both learning how many families within their relatively affluent community are surprisingly in need of food. They were both contributing to a solution to a serious problem and the other child has learned a more appropriate way to satisfy her hunger.

The best consequences may be unpleasant and/or make the child feel uncomfortable, but their primary mission is to teach a better or less harmful way to satisfy the physical or emotional needs that are often at the root of a problem behavior.

## Questions for Reflection

1. What is the primary goal of a consequence?

2. Why is it important to notice and appreciate our kids when they are behaving appropriately?

3. What are the most effective ways to give a reward?

4. Why should we try to avoid yelling when we are upset with our child? When is it okay to raise our voice?

5. If a neighbor or teacher complained to you about something your child said or did, what would you do next?

# CHAPTER 7

# Communicating Effectively with Your Kids

*As your kids grow, they may forget what you said but they won't forget how you made them feel.*

—KEVIN HEATH

WE ARE BEST ABLE TO INFLUENCE OUR CHILDREN WHEN WE EFFECtively communicate our thoughts and feelings, and demonstrate a deep understanding of theirs. Kids without such support are vulnerable to the loudest, most appealing and seductive voice, or to the drive for pleasure and instant gratification. We communicate in a variety of ways. While words and language are important, tone of voice, body language, and facial expression transmit more than 90 percent of a meaningful message. Therefore, *how* we say something and our demeanor while we *listen* are the two most critical elements.

## KEYS TO GOOD LISTENING

Listening is a difficult skill to master. My wife often told our children that they have two ears and only one mouth for a reason: to listen at least twice as much as they talk. There are multiple benefits when we listen effectively to our children:

- We show children that we care.

- We dignify children by showing that we respect their questions and views.
- We give children a chance to express their thoughts and feelings.
- We let children know they are important.
- We model self-control by showing that we pay attention before acting.

*Make time.* It could be helpful to set aside a few minutes every day as "listening time" although kids tend to be most spontaneous on their own terms. They are more apt to initiate conversation while being driven to the soccer game, taking a bike ride, or eating an after-school snack. Look at those times together as opportunities to connect rather than demands you have to fulfill.

Even when a child has no apparent need to talk, get in the habit of sharing daily. You can start by sharing something about your workday or an event that caught your interest and then asking your child about his. Ask a specific question like, "What was the best thing that happened to you at school today?" rather than "How was school?"

A good conversation starter can get kids to share meaningful events and experiences, leading to more than one-word answers like "okay" or "good."

Appendix A contains a list of different questions parents and teachers can ask every day to start a conversation. Be sure not to try to engage when they are playing video games, watching television, listening to music, trying to avoid an unpleasant task, or are otherwise preoccupied. As well, ask when you really want to know. Don't ask your child about her day when you are distracted or preoccupied with your own. Our kids will want to talk to us when they know that we really want to hear what they have to say.

Similarly, like a stranger who greets you with, "How's it going?" but really has no interest or time to truly hear what you have to say, asking your child some version of "How was school today?" is likely to get you one-word answers when you have other things on your mind. After you ask a question, make good eye contact and paraphrase what you just heard to ensure understanding or to have your child clarify (see *Active Listen*).

Teachers can learn a lot about their students by occasionally eating lunch with individuals or small groups.

*Concentrate and focus.* Since good listening requires concentration, try not to compete with the many distractions around us, such as a blaring television, incoming text messages, a ringing telephone, or something cooking in the oven. Empty other thoughts from your head, so they don't interfere with what you are hearing. Before you speak, take a breath. If you miss something, it is better to ask the child to repeat it than to pretend that you heard. For example, you might say something like: "Sorry. I was zoning out. Would you say that again?" or "I missed what you said. Would you mind repeating it?"

*Active Listen.* When your child expresses strong positive or negative feelings and/or uncertainty about how to handle a situation, encourage her to talk more about what is going on. Active listening can be a very helpful tool to guide your child in those situations. After your child shares, paraphrase what was said in your own words to ensure understanding (e.g., "*What I hear you saying* is you think your coach is unfair and doesn't like you. Did I hear you correctly?"). When you want to express understanding but nothing is coming easily, make eye contact and nod your head or use words like "Oh," "I see," "No kidding," "Really," and "Hmm," followed by, "Is there anything else you want to say about that?"

**Suggestion:** Practice active listening with a partner (e.g., your spouse, a friend, or a colleague). Ask your partner a question like "Tell me about the best part and least favorite part of your day."

After your partner completes a thought, practice repeating back the experiences and feelings that stand out the most (e.g., "So it sounds like you felt [disappointed, upset, frustrated, excited, motivated, happy, sad] when s/he said/did [identify the experience or event].")." "Did I miss anything?" Some kids will continue on and go deeper without prompting. Others may not. If you have questions about what you just heard, ask for clarification. For example, "I'm a little confused," or, "I want to make sure I fully understand." End with something like "Tell me more about_____."

*Ask probing questions rather than giving answers.* To be sure you understand and to give your child a chance to delve or reflect more, ask a thought-provoking question such as, "Can you think of any reasons your teacher might be upset with you?" If the child seems unaware, offer your hunches. For example, "A few teachers are just angry people that you have to learn to deal with, but most who get upset at students are reacting to those who don't do their work or are rude or who disrupt class. Some get frustrated when they think a kid doesn't care enough to do as well as s/he could. What do you think might be going on with your teacher toward you?"

Follow that with, "So can you think of some ways that might get the teacher to pick on you less or to be more fair?" After you listen, share your ideas. For example, "I have a few ideas that I think might work well. Would you like to hear what they are?"

*Thank your child.* Many issues will recur and may need to be discussed or revisited again (sometimes several times). However, when an end point has been reached for now, conclude by summarizing and thanking your child for sharing (e.g., "Thanks for sharing. I feel good about your plan to say 'good morning' with a smile on your face every day for the next week to see if that gets your teacher to be nicer to you. Is there anything else I missed that you plan to do?").

*Explore sensitive subjects.* It can feel awkward for parents to bring up certain sensitive topics like sex, drugs, and other potentially harmful behaviors or for your child to share troubling thoughts and feelings they may be having but are too uncomfortable to initiate. Yet it is extremely important to be attuned to issues and troubles that most kids can become very adept at hiding when they don't want you to know. For example, it is not unusual for even the most attentive parents to miss warning signs in children who have either attempted or committed suicide. One way to stay current with what and how your child may be thinking and feeling is by **indirectly** bringing up these topics:

- I saw a show today about kids who (topic). Have you ever thought about that? Do you ever hear other kids talking about that?
- I read online today about how youth suicide has been increasing. Is that something that is ever talked about at school?
- I was surprised to hear that even kids as young as ten or eleven are vaping. Do you know what that means? Does that go on at your school? Is that something that has ever crossed your mind?
- I read an article today about kids whose reputations have been harmed by online rumors and other nasty stuff said about them that may or may not be true. Does any of that happen when you are online?

*If your child won't talk and you don't know why, wonder aloud and start with you.* There may be times when something that is troubling to your child is unclear to both him/her and you. At least one but maybe neither of you know exactly what is going on but you've noticed more agitation, frustration, or withdrawal. At those times, I have found it helpful to open the door by starting with myself. For example,

"Bill, you've been especially quiet lately. You used to seem happier but more and more you seem distant and it's worrying me. Is there something going on that's bothering you (pause for an answer)?"

If none, wonder aloud:

"I'm wondering if maybe I did something to bother you or if something is going on with a friend or at school or somewhere else. Talk to me."

If little or no response, or you continue to suspect something is not right, continue aloud:

"When I don't want to talk, it's usually because I don't think they really want to understand what I think or how I feel. Other times, I might feel embarrassed or uneasy. Just so you know, there is nothing and nobody I care about and want to understand more than you (if you are a teacher 'all of my students'). So what's going on?"

If little or no response,

"Know that my door is always open to listen and help."

**Suggestion:** This is another situation in which it might be wise to seek feedback from others who know or regularly interact with your child and/or from a mental health professional at school or in the community (e.g., teacher, guidance counselor, close friend of your child).

*Use a scale to get your child to identify mood and feelings.* When I was recently in the hospital following elective surgery, every caregiver began the conversation by asking me to rate my pain on a scale of 1 to 10. This is a good technique to use with your children when you want to quickly know how they are being affected by something or to let them know how you are being affected by something. For example, "Shawna, on a scale of 1 to 10 with 1 being the worst (least) and 10 being the best (most), how would you rate your_____?" The scale can be used to rate happiness, disappointment, degree of difficulty, likeability, worry, confidence, embarrassment, interest, enthusiasm, feelings about, etc.

*When your child is disappointed about a performance.* If your child plays a sport or sings in a show and didn't do as well as they would have liked, take your cue from the child. If there is silence right after the game or performance, probably s/he does not want to talk about it right then. Most kids know when they had a bad game or performance; some are simply exhausted; and many just want to be temporarily alone with their thoughts. They don't want to re-live the experience right then. Offer your opinion or advice only if you are asked.

Some youngsters want to talk about it right away, and they will. Just listen. Some will make a statement or ask a question ("Can you believe how I messed up?"; "Do you think I should have caught the ball? I was so close!") Before you offer an opinion, focus on effort and attitude (e.g., "Sometimes, getting close is as close as you can get. If you tried your best right then, there is nothing more you could have done. Take a few deep breaths now because I know you're disappointed, and let's talk again about that play later if you want or ask your coach if s/he thinks there is anything you could do differently if that play happens again.).

## Getting kids to listen to You

A private conversation that offers specific feedback presented in a dignified way and seeks a plan for improvement when necessary, earns respect without fear. When teaching, explaining, or correcting your child, the same advice applies.

**Suggestion:** Begin with "I" when you share your thoughts and feelings. "I" statements provide a way to let your child know clearly and specifically how and why you feel as you do. You own your feelings making it easier for a child to hear what you say. A "you" message conveys some combination of lecture, criticism, sarcasm, threat, or scolding. Even when these messages work to stop misbehavior, they often have the negative effect of eroding a child's self-esteem. Notice the differences in the examples below:

"YOU" MESSAGES

Phillip, knock it off! Keep your hands off the expensive furniture. If you don't stop, you'll be sorry!

Anna, your loud laughing and silliness are driving me crazy. Talk like the big girl you are, not like a baby.

How many times do I have to tell you to pick your stuff up, Juan?!

Latoya, your poor grade is because you didn't put in the work. You would do better if you tried harder.

## "I" STATEMENTS

Phillip, I am worried that rough touching will scratch and ruin the expensive furniture. Please touch gently or not at all.

Anna, I'm working with the reading group, and I need to have quiet so I can hear them read. Thanks for your help.

Juan, leaving your stuff lying around creates clutter and I worry that before long someone is going to trip and possibly get hurt. Please pick up your stuff.

Latoya, I am disappointed to see the poor grade, especially since it seems you hardly studied. How do you plan to change that beginning today?

*Monitor messages that your child is hearing and seeing.* Commit to spending at least one hour each week watching the television shows, exploring the video games, and listening to some of the same music that your kids are hearing. It's a great way to stay connected and current.

Be aware of your child's time on the internet. Knowing the kinds of things that are influencing your child, can better prepare you to communicate effectively with her. You don't have to pretend to like it, and in fact if you don't, use your feelings as a springboard to discuss issues and values that are important to you. For example, "I like the rhythm of that song but those lyrics sound violent to me. Do you hear it that way?"

Since each generation seems to invent its own language and adopt its own music, plead your ignorance and ask for explanations (e.g., "I don't understand what's cool about that video game. What am I missing?"). Kids love to feel that they know more than their parents or teachers. Let them teach you!

*Apologize when you blow it and know it.* My father was a loving man but he also had an explosive temper that frightened me. Although I had a lot of respect and love for him, to this day I remember that he NEVER apologized for anything he ever said or did and I resented him a lot for that. I think it took me much longer for us to make peace because of that. In fact, rarely do I remember what caused the conflict, but I have no trouble remembering that days would often go by before we did. Maybe he didn't think it was wrong to occasionally freak out and act irrationally or maybe he was just too proud to apologize.

Although most parents and teachers would agree that screaming or losing our temper is best avoided, our stresses and fears may lead us to say or do things we later regret. None of us are perfect. Despite efforts to listen and express ourselves effectively, there are times when our buttons are pushed and we may react angrily or impulsively. When we realize that our response has been inappropriate, there is everything right about apologizing.

Be careful about soaking yourself in guilt, because if you do, you might end up negating an important moment of correction that your child needs. Although there might have been a better method of correction, if this loss of control was very rare for you, simply apologize in a forthright way and explain why this issue triggered your anger. For example, "Liam, even though I was and still am very disappointed in what you did, it wasn't right for me to say some of the nasty things that I did. I apologize for raising my voice and talking to you in a hurtful way. Now that you know how I feel, I want to share why and how I expect better from you. Is now a good time?" You will want to follow up with a planning or problem-solving strategy that addresses the issue.

Apologizing to our kids gives more meaning when we suggest they apologize to others for their transgressions.

**Suggestions:** The next time you think your child should apologize for doing something unacceptable, start by apologizing first. For example, John hits and pushes his three-year-old brother who wandered into his room and messed up his trains. Rather than telling John to apologize for hitting or pushing, Mom first says to John, "Your brother needs to learn not to come into your room and start messing around with your stuff. I let him know that what he did was wrong and he must apologize to you for doing that. Now that you know what he should apologize for doing, what else could you have done besides hit him?"

As already noted but worth speating, Yelling, screaming, swearing, hitting, or otherwise losing self-control are never justifiable responses to a child with the possible exception of use in an emergency (like a child running into a street). It is otherwise an expression of frustration with the child or much more often, with unsatisfactory life circumstances for which others pay a steep emotional price. Don't let pride or denial get in the way of help. Apologies are essential but not enough. You may be unable to erase the past, but you can learn how to prevent the cycle of unharnessed anger from continuing to damage those you love.

You must take responsibility for what you did, try to explain your problem to those injured as best you can (there is no good explanation), and do serious work on eliminating your violence. For example, "I had no right to (say directly what you did). You never deserve the hurt I cause and I know this is not the first time, but even once is too much. I wish I could take it back, but I can't. The best I can do is tell you that this is a big problem for me and I am going to quickly find (name a counselor or organization) to learn better ways to control myself."

*Bring up tough issues.* At younger and younger ages, our kids know more than we often want to believe about sensitive issues like bullying, sex, and drugs. Although many of us would prefer to bury our heads in the sand, our kids may need help processing these issues.

Bring up issues that you think are relevant to your child. For example, "I remember when I was in school, there were a couple of kids that got bullied a lot. I hated seeing it but I was torn between wanting to say something to make it stop yet worried that if I did, the bully would pick on me. Does that sort of thing happen at your school? Has that ever happened to you? What do you think you might do if you were in that situation?"

When my sons were teenagers, they asked if I had ever used drugs. Startled, I initially grew silent while my heart pounded away. At first, I asked them why they wanted to know, which led to a good conversation. I wound up acknowledging that I had smoked marijuana occasionally when I was younger because some of my friends did and I was curious to know how it would make me feel. In addition, I told them that I considered myself lucky because some people I knew wound up getting addicted and it is impossible to predict who will and who won't. I then asked if they had tried any drugs and both confided that they had tried marijuana and alcohol but they didn't like it. I did not make them promise that they would never use drugs or avoid hanging out with people who did, but I did invite them to talk to me at any time about this or anything else without fearing judgment.

Our kids need straight talk from those who love them. Some studies have shown that kids who talk to their parents about drugs are half as likely to use them as kids who don't (Turnbridge, 2022). They are much more likely to reveal themselves to you when they know you don't avoid discussing sensitive issues. Try to keep things in perspective. On two separate occasions when my daughter was in high school, she came home very drunk. After the second time, my wife called a few of her friends and we had her evaluated for alcoholism. Afterward, we felt reassured that her drinking was rare and at least temporarily in control. However, there were consequences for her.

If you suspect your child is involved in behaviors that can lead to serious problems, do not sit and suffer in silence, but also don't freak out. Express your concern and explore further. Do not worry about violating privacy. There can be no privacy when it comes to concerns you have about behaviors that *may* put your child's health or well-being at risk. Be specific and give your child a chance to be honest, although don't expect that s/he will. For example, "Ben, I am concerned that your grades have gone down and your eyes seem bloodshot to me. Are you using?" No matter the answer, talk about your concerns with a school or community professional.

## QUESTIONS FOR REFLECTION

1. Identify at least a few minutes every day to listen to each of your children about their day. What "conversation starters" can you use (see Appendix A)?

2. What are two ways you can listen more effectively to your child and two ways you can get your child to listen to you?

3. How might you change a "you" message of blame to an "I" statement that teaches?

4. What tough issues are your kids likely to experience but reluctant to bring to your attention? How might you invite them to talk to you about these issues?

5. When was the last time you apologized to a child for behaving inappropriately? If not, what kept you from doing so shortly after the incident?

# Helping Your Kids Solve People Problems

*Too often we give our children answers to problems rather than problems to solve.*

—ROGER LEWIN

THERE ARE OFTEN COMPETING DESIRES IN LIFE THAT MAKE MANY DECI-sions difficult even at the earliest ages. Watching my three-year-old grandson waver between the excitement of dipping his feet in the inviting ocean and running away from the crashing waves as they approached offers a simple example. Many conflicts are far more complex to untangle: what to do about brothers, sisters, or other children who hit or tease; handling the disappointment of not making the grade, special class, or team; managing peer pressure; getting along with insensitive teachers and bosses; responding to bullies.

We can best prepare our children to deal with these issues by showing and teaching them how to make decisions that give them what they need safely without hurting others.

**SIX STEPS TO HELP YOUR CHILD SOLVE PROBLEMS AND MAKE GOOD DECISIONS**

1. *Use your child's discomfort to start problem solving.* Like adults, children are uncomfortable when they have a problem. Somebody just took something of theirs, they got into trouble at school, they

weren't invited to a party, they got a poor grade on the test, they struck out in the baseball game. Begin by expressing your empathy. For example, "You weren't invited to the sleepover and you are feeling hurt. Is that right?" Then listen until the child seems finished expressing her or his feelings.

2. *Ask what the problem is.* Encourage your child to state the problem aloud. Afterward, it can often help to use your own words to summarize. For example, "So it sounds like you are feeling left out, especially since you haven't met a new group of girls that make you feel comfortable since we moved. Is that what's going on?"

3. *Guide but don't give a solution.* Guard against the parental instinct to solve the problem. Instead ask, "Do you have any ideas about how you might make some new friends?" If your child seems bewildered, offer an idea to get things moving: "How do you think it might be if you invited one or more of the girls here for a sleepover on a different night? Does that sound like something that might work or do you have some other ideas?"

4. *Encourage "emptying out."* When your child seems finished offering possible solutions, ask, "Is there anything else?" a few times before moving on.

5. *Help choose a solution if necessary.* This is where they need to consider which choice(s) will best achieve their goal. For example, "So what sounds best to you?" (If the child thinks it is best to quit the activity or avoid a temporarily uncomfortable experience, say something like "I know you would rather just not ask anybody to sleep over because you wouldn't want to feel hurt if they said no. But then you would feel lonely. So if you decided to take a risk and call someone, who would that be?"

6. *Identify a back-up plan in case of the "what ifs."* For example, "Inviting Emily for a sleepover sounds like a great idea. But just in case she's busy, who else might you ask or what else might you do to not feel lonely?"

## SOLVING PROBLEMS WITH PEERS

*Sibling Bickering.* There is no such thing as the always-happy family that consistently solves its problems smoothly and happily with the welfare of all in mind. Problems between siblings are inevitable and are often a good topic for family or problem-solving meetings, discussed in detail later in this chapter. On a regular basis, each child needs special time with a parent independent of siblings. Among other things, it can provide an opportunity to discuss important issues that can include sibling conflict while helping your child become better at problem solving by using the six steps previously mentioned.

When sibling bickering is persistent, you might try to make a habit of appreciating and noticing (no cost rewards p.66) when they are getting along well. When children are quick to blame each other, redirect their attention to how they may be contributing to the problem. For example, "Even if he did start it, how did you add to it? What else can you do right now if you want it to stop?"

*Handling bullies.* While growing up, significant numbers of children are targeted for bullying and ridicule by peers. In fact, it is difficult to get through adolescence without having been victimized along the way. This includes spreading rumors as well as putdowns of family, appearance, intelligence, ethnicity, or any personal characteristic. As a child, I remember being targeted by two boys in my class who would whisper to each other in my presence, then smirk at me while imitating some of my gestures. I remember simultaneously feeling afraid and angry. Fortunately, like most, it didn't last for very long and I don't remember doing anything special to make it stop. I must have continued with my activities, hung out with friends, and avoided these kids whenever I could. Eventually, they must have either found someone else to pick on or maybe they turned on each other. That said, there are some kids who are continuously bullied with suicide being the most tragic consequence.

Sometimes the bullying includes physical aggression. Nowadays, it is often done electronically. Kids with strong friendships are less frequently targeted, and even when they are, it is easier to ward off the bully when kids can get support from their peers. So as a parent, you want to do all you can to encourage your child to seek relationships with other kids. That said, specific suggestions and skills we can provide our children when they are targeted follow. Practice is required for kids to use these strategies effectively. To demonstrate, ask your child to pretend to be the bully and you play the role of victim. Then switch roles. Many children will require lots of practice to get comfortable with these methods, especially the few that are unusual or counterintuitive.

### 1. Ignore and Walk Away.

This is the advice most parents give their child. The key is to avoid giving the bully an emotional payoff. Reacting with tears, fear, or anger usually just spurs on the bully. Explain that to your child (e.g., "If you show the bully that s/ he can make you upset with words or actions, they will keep doing the same thing. It is better to stay calm and act like you aren't both- ered."). Acknowledge how difficult it may be to just ignore or walk away after someone says or does something mean but that it is usually the best thing to do several times because it usually works but sometimes it doesn't. Let's practice.

### 2. The "name change" strategy.

To make it a bit easier to ignore and walk away, teach your child the "name change" strategy. For example, say, "When (bully) laughed and called you *stupid*, you got upset. What if instead, (bully) had called you a *pencil*, would you have cried? Would you get upset? If (bully) called you an *apple*, does that make you an apple? Don't you think it would probably be pretty easy to stay calm and maybe even laugh, ignore, and/or walk away? So (use as many examples as you think are needed). How about trying that the next time (bully) says or does (behavior)? See if it becomes any easier to just ignore and walk away. Is that something you might want to try?"

### 3. Teach skills of assertion.

When ignoring doesn't work, teach your child to make eye contact, and with as few words as possible, *calmly* (use the strategy above) tell the bully to stop. Have your child prac- tice saying something like, "Stop," "Enough," "I don't like it," "I'm sick of it." Then have her practice walking away.

<u>4. Agree with the put-down.</u>

Teach your child the Roxanne technique. An old Steve Martin movie, *ROXANNE*, contains one of the best examples of handling put-downs I have ever seen. Steve Martin plays the large-nosed Cyrano de Bergerac character. At one point, he goes into a bar and is immediately greeted with a variety of put-downs about his looks by a group of bullies. He responds to each insult by agreeing and exaggerating. Here is an example:

*Bully:* Look at that nose. Can you believe how big it is?

*Victim:* I know. It's about as big as can be.

*Bully:* Yeah. If I had a nose like that, I'd want to hide all day.

*Victim:* For sure! I wouldn't blame you. It's even bigger than a fire hose.

When they all laugh at him, he joins the laughter and laughs the loudest. Eventually, they stop because they can't outdo his "self-put-downs" and calm demeanor. Agreeing and even exaggerating can provide children with a protective shield. I recall Nikki, a second-grade student who was teased by a group of girls who made fun of her buck teeth by calling her "bucky." With practice, Nikki learned to smile and calmly say, "You're right. I wish I had teeth just like yours."

To practice, begin by asking your child to take on the role of the bully and act toward you the same way the bully is with your child. Demonstrate and then teach answering each put-down with one of the following, ending with walking away, changing seats, or otherwise creat- ing distance if possible:

*You can think that if you want.*
*Thanks for letting me know.*
*You might be right.*

For example:

*Your child (as the bully):* You smell like a dead fish.

*You (as your child):* You can think that if you want. It's a free country.

*Your child (as the bully):* Why don't you take a shower?

*You (as your child):* Thanks for the suggestion.

*Your child (as the bully):* You are really stupid.

*You (as your child):* You might be right.

Some kids may be unable to walk away, especially if there is an audience of other kids watching. They may worry about how they look to peers if they simply agree. When that is the case, teach them to add four words at the end, *but I don't agree.*

### 5. Learn strategies of physical self-defense.

Bullied kids should be encouraged to learn the art of self-defense through martial arts. This often builds self-esteem and confidence, which takes a huge hit when kids are bullied. It will often give your child the confidence s/he needs to more effectively use the strategies identified above.

### 6. Get help when necessary.

If being bullied is a persistent pattern, you will need to intercede with proper school or community authorities. Most states have enacted anti-bullying laws, and most schools are now required to have a policy and procedures that address this serious issue.

*Be available to take the blame.* Peer pressure is a powerful dynamic that can get kids into trouble. Encourage them to blame you as an excuse if and when they are in uncomfortable situations, feeling pressure to conform, are up against a more powerful foe, and are looking for a way out but need to "save face." For example, one influential teen says to a few friends, "Let's go get drunk." Other kids join in and say "Yeah", but your kid doesn't want to. S/he feels pressure to conform but wants a way out. Practice "lines" with them such as:

- "I'd love to go but my mother will kill me if she finds out and I'm not ready to die yet. But thanks anyway."
- "That sounds really cool and I wish I could, but if I did, I'd never see the car again."
- "Nah (No), but thanks for the invite."
- "Wow, if my parents were cool, I would. But they are a royal pain in the a—!"
- "Man, much as I wish I could, I gotta get home and take care of my annoying sister! But have a good time without me."

## FAMILY MEETINGS

Weekly family meetings with all family members present for 30 minutes to an hour can be a very useful structure in which problems can be identified and possible solutions offered, particularly among families that rarely eat dinner together. During the preschool years, meetings of just a few minutes are appropriate. This is also a time when daily or weekly highlights (good things that have happened or good deeds done for others) can be shared. At first, the parent(s) leads meetings, but later on, responsibility for leadership can be shared with children. The following process can help parents plan and organize these meetings.

*Express Gratitude.* A good way to begin meetings is to have each family member share one or two things for which they feel thankful that have happened since they last met. With all the competing demands in the lives of children and adults, this enables all family members to catch up.

*Share appreciations.* Ask each family member to share at least one nice thing about each other that enriched their lives during the week ("I like what you did [said] when you_____.").

*Raise issues for problem-solving.* Make a list of issues any or all members may want to discuss ("Who's got something they'd like to talk about?"). This can include just about anything that ranges from ideas and discussion about a family vacation to concerns about oneself, the behavior(s) of other family or friends, problems with other family members. With the exception of possible danger (e.g., suicidal thoughts or plans, drug use, possession of a weapon, gang involvement), all outside issues may only be discussed with permission of the specific individual (e.g., poor grades, peer problems, feelings about outsiders).

*Discuss and decide.* Discuss and decide which problems are most appropriate with all family present and which ones are best addressed at another time or in a different setting. When a problem is chosen for discussion, all are encouraged to share their ideas. Before the meeting ends, each problem is discussed and solved, or an alternative plan is developed that identifies when or how the problem will get solved.

## SOME POSSIBLE ISSUES FOR FAMILY MEETINGS

- Ted keeps walking into my room without knocking.
- I think it is unfair that I do all of the chores and nobody else around here helps out.
- There's a kid at school who is really scary!
- Joey keeps taking my toys. Then he hits me when I try to get them back.
- The trip to Grandma's house is at the same time as my hockey game.

- On the bus (internet; at lunch), a few girls keep teasing and saying mean things that aren't true about Lily (friend). I don't know how we can get them to stop!

## WIN-WIN PROBLEM SOLVING THROUGH NEGOTIATION

Negotiation is discussion and compromise when two or more people are in conflict about something that affects them. It is the singular most effective strategy when raising insistent, demanding children who are as persistent and strong-willed as a bulldog. Parents of these children constantly face the dilemma of what to address and what to ignore. Otherwise, every little thing can turn into an exhausting power struggle. You must choose your battles wisely.

Without question, all matters related to *health* and *safety* should be considered non-negotiable and require parents to stand their ground. Naturally, if your child is engaging in harmful behavior either to himself or others, you will need to do whatever is necessary, including proper and safe restraints, even if it means enduring frequent "meltdowns." Some children have extreme difficulty coping with changes to their routine and do much better when provided a daily schedule.

Many incidents can avoid escalation by framing demands as choices (e.g., "Would it be more helpful to get yourself dressed or for me to get you started?"). With many other issues, the goal is to find common ground that everyone can live with. Negotiations can be brief or extensive. Below is an example of a parent introducing the idea of negotiation to her child:

*Parent:* Do you know what the word "compromise" means?

*Joey:* Sort of. Like when you try to agree to do something that you don't really want to do.

*Parent:* Yeah. It's when two or more people want different things and they both work hard to make sure both get at least some of what they each want.

*Joey:* Huh?

*Parent:* Like if I want you to go to bed at 9 o'clock but you want to go to bed at 11 o'clock, what would be in the middle?

*Joey:* 10 o'clock?

*Parent:* Right. Neither of us would be getting exactly what we think is best but we would try to find a solution that we could each live with. Does that make sense?

*Joey:* Sure.

*Parent:* Okay. Let's try a different one. Let's say you and your sister both want to watch TV at the same time but you want to watch different programs. What would be a compromise?

*Joey:* How about if we each had our own TV.

*Parent:* That would be great if we had a lot of money, but we don't. So let's see if we can think of a different solution.

*Joey:* (becoming impatient) I don't know.

*Parent:* How about if you watched your show on Monday and she watched hers on Tuesday.

*Joey:* But I want to watch my show every day.

*Parent:* Well, how about you watch your show on Monday and we record your show on Tuesday while she is watching hers. Then you can watch your show right after you wake up on Wednesday morning. Do you see how that could be a compromise?

*Joey:* Yeah.

When compromise seems unlikely, the parent has no way to track or monitor a child's behavior, and it is free from danger, it is usually best to let go. Avoid conflict. For example:

*Sarah:* I am sleeping over at Jane's house tonight.

*Parent:* Last time you stayed over there, you came home exhausted the next day and had trouble getting your homework done.

*Sarah:* (agitated) There you go again! You never let me do what I want. I'm not a baby, and I'm sleeping over!

*Parent:* (seeking compromise) Hold on. I'm not saying you can't, I'm just saying I'd like you to promise to go to sleep by 12 so you are not so tired tomorrow.

*Sarah:* I think that's stupid. I can decide and I will.

*Parent:* (deciding this is not an issue of danger or worth a meltdown) You know, Sarah, I think you are right. You are mature enough to decide. How about you promise *to try* to get a good night's sleep?

*Sarah:* Okay.

## A NEGOTIATION BETWEEN MOTHER AND YOUNG CHILD

Notice that the mother provides clues and *suggestions* for her young child.

*Mother:* Janie, I am upset that you keep taking stuff out of my purse without asking. Do you understand what I'm saying?

*Janie:* Yes, Mom.

*Mother:* You have done this more than once even though I have asked you not to. What are you looking for?

*Janie:* I wish I had some makeup that I could play with sometimes.

*Mother:* Are you happy when I let you play with my old makeup kit?

*Janie:* Yes, I like it when you give me that kind of stuff.

*Mother:* I'm willing to buy you some play makeup and sometimes let you use my old stuff, if you ask. What do I want you to do?

*Janie:* I guess I won't take things out of your purse anymore.

*Mother:* I am glad to hear that, but I also want you to ask when you want something that belongs to me.

*Janie:* Okay, I promise to ask.

*Mother:* Okay, I promise to buy you that kid's makeup next weekend.

*Three days later*

*Mother:* I'm very happy that you haven't gone into my purse. Yesterday you asked if you could use my old makeup. I'm really glad you acted like a big girl and waited rather than whined when I said you could but only after dinner.

## NEGOTIATION BETWEEN AN OLDER CHILD AND FATHER

The following negotiation enables both father and his son to deepen their understanding of an issue and each other to set in motion long-lasting change.

*Father:* I really get angry that you complain and make faces when I don't agree with you. *(I message)*

*Elliot:* But you always say "no" unless I explain where I'm going, who I'll be hanging out with, and exactly what time I have to be home. I'm not a little kid anymore.

*Father:* So you think I ask too many questions and maybe don't trust you enough to make good decisions on your own? *(Active listen)*

*Elliot:* Exactly.

*Father:* Okay. You want more freedom to go places and do things without always having to tell me. Is that how it is? *(More active listen)*

*Elliot:* Yeah.

*Father:* It's not that I don't trust you, and I think it is fair for you to want to make more decisions on your own. I just worry when I don't know where you are because I love you. Let's think about how you can feel more independent and I can know you're safe. *(Problem-Solving)*

With rare exception, encourage the child to offer possible solutions first since any that are acceptable to you will give him/her a greater sense of control, which is often at the root of an adult-child conflict. Remember to use the "emptying out" strategy.

Father and Elliot share their thoughts and agree that when Elliot goes out, he will tell where he plans to go or do and when he will be home. If worried, Father can call but no more than twice. Elliot agrees to call Father and let him know of any change in plans before making them.

## NEGOTIATION BETWEEN KIDS

Mother serves as a *mediator* in this negotiation to help two of her children resolve a dispute. Notice how she leads them to share *dislikes, likes, wants,* and *solutions* with each other.

*Mom:* Okay, Jennifer and Danny. You both seem so angry with each other. Let's talk about it because I am tired of listening to the bickering.

Tell each other what is making you mad (*Mother has to make sure that each child shares without being interrupted by the other*). How about if Jennifer goes first, but remember you both will have lots of turns.

*Jennifer:* He took my book and won't give it back.

*Danny:* Not true. She took my Gameboy without asking.

*Mom:* It's Jennifer's turn. You don't have to agree, Danny. Just listen. You'll get your turn when she's done.

*Jennifer:* Danny, you took my book without asking.

*Mom:* Danny, please tell Jennifer what she is angry about.

*Danny:* I didn't do anything first.

*Mom:* Just tell her what she is angry about. You don't have to agree, but you do have to understand why the other person gets annoyed. (*Each child is expected to repeat the complaint they just heard to make sure they understand each other.*)

*Danny:* Okay. You're mad that I took your book.

*Mom:* Now, Danny, tell Jennifer what you are angry about.

*Danny:* She took my game without asking.

*Mom:* Tell her.

*Danny:* You took my game.

*Mom:* Jennifer, tell Danny what he is angry about.

*Jennifer:* I took your game without permission.

*Mom:* Jennifer, now tell Danny something he does that you like (*to build a foundation of good will, each side is asked to share something they appreciate about the other person*).

*Jennifer:* That's hard.

*Mom:* Try hard.

*Jennifer:* You came to my show at school and cheered me on.

*Mom:* Danny, tell Jennifer what she liked.

*Danny:* You liked that I went to your show.

*Mom:* Now your turn, Danny. What does Jennifer do that you like?

*Danny:* You helped me out at the Ninja Warrior factory. I like going there with you.

*Mom:* Next, I want you to tell what you want each other to do differently so that there is less bickering. Who wants to go first? (*Each side says what they want the other to do differently.*)

*Jennifer:* Don't take my stuff without asking.

*Mom:* Now you, Danny.

*Danny:* Don't take my stuff without asking.

Mom: Now you both know what you like and don't like. You both know what you want. What are you willing to do to help solve the problem? (*Both sides negotiate until a solution is reached.*)

*Danny:* I won't take your stuff without asking.

*Jennifer:* I won't take your stuff without asking.

*Mom*: Okay, sounds like you are each going to respect the other person by asking before taking. I'm glad and proud that both of you found a way to solve the problem. We will get together in a couple of days and see how it's going (*a time for follow-up is scheduled to see how things are working*).

Before ending, Mom asks each of them **how** they will ask each other if they want to borrow an item and what they will each do if either says "no." After a satisfactory solution that likely avoids more conflict because of a "no," the meeting is ended:

*Mom*: We will get together in a couple of days and see how it's going (a time for follow-up is scheduled to see how things are working).

Making your home a place where negotiation is regularly used to handle disagreements gives your children the advantage of learning how to effectively communicate and understand the perspective of other people. Keep in mind that it is not necessary to have time-consuming negotiations to solve most problems. Use these processes primarily to help solve problems that frequently recur. Otherwise, use them as needed.

Educators or trained students can serve as mediators when two or more students of equivalent stature are in conflict at school.

## QUESTIONS FOR REFLECTION

1. What does your child do or not do that annoys you but isn't that important? How would it feel if you decided to let your child "win" that battle?

2. What are the six steps to good decision making and problem solving?

3. What are some issues within your family that you might try to solve at a "family meeting"?

4. What is one issue you have with your child that you will attempt to reach compromise with negotiation?

5. How might you serve as a mediator with two or more of your children to help them negotiate a problem between them?

# CHAPTER 9

# What To Do When Kids Push Your Buttons

*Actions speak louder than words.*

—A PROVERB WE'VE ALL HEARD

UNTIL I HAD MY OWN KIDS, I COULDN'T REALLY UNDERSTAND HOW ANY parent could harm their child at all, much less to the extreme of "shaken baby syndrome." While I still have little sympathy for adults who lose control, I can totally understand how the frustration of being unable to console an infant, re-direct a "badgering child," or maintain self-control when treated with disrespect can at times feel overwhelming. When our kids say or do things that fray our nerves or that we find personally offensive, what actions and words can help us handle things safely and effectively?

## LISTEN BEYOND THE WORD OR DEED

It is highly likely that your child will at least occasionally express frustration with some combination of angry, unappreciative, obnoxious, annoying, and disrespectful words or deeds. At these moments, it is normal to feel disappointed and angry. Don't fight fire with more fire. If you can't stay calm, excuse yourself and re-connect later. For example, "Joe, you have a right to feel the way you do, but I'm not your punching bag.

When you can talk to me without swearing, I'll do my best to listen." Then walk away.

As upset or startled as you may be, keep in mind that the child is primarily expressing pain, anger, or fear. It is not helpful to react with phrases like "What did you say?!" or "After all I do for you, how dare you talk to me like that!" Responses like those usually cause the child to either shut down or escalate.

The best way to teach kids to "stop and think" before they emotionally react is to avoid "knee-jerk" reacting in a way you may later regret. If you allow the stress, frustration, and anger you may feel to take charge by giving in to bad behavior or freaking out because of it, things will only get worse.

Instead, view this difficult moment as an opportunity to model appropriate ways to calm down before attempting to solve a problem. If need be, rather than allowing unfiltered anger to take control, tell your child how you feel and what you are going to do to take care of yourself. For example, "I am not your punching bag and I will not tolerate your yelling and disrespectful words. Before I say or do something I don't mean, I'm going to walk away and take a few deep breaths to calm down. You might want to do that as well." Then do what you need to do to calm yourself down (see chapter 11). Learn to not take offensive behavior personally because rarely is it. Try to get outside yourself. Accept the moment for what it is.

Later on, get with your child and deal with the issue. For example, "I know you were very upset and I want to understand what is bothering you, but I can't listen when you yell angry words at me. Now that we are both calmer, let's see if we can solve the problem in a better way."

## THREE POWERFUL WORDS THAT DEFUSE

When a child's words or actions cross the line, it is usually sufficient to confront the behavior by saying, "That was disrespectful." Pause for a moment and then ask, "Is that what you meant?" Most kids will say "no." Follow with reminders about how to say things more appropriately (e.g., "I am sorry to hear that I may have done something to upset you, but you may not yell or swear at me! If you want to talk more about it, I'll listen when your voice is calm and your words are respectful."). Then walk away.

## Quick one-liners

There are many things to say in the heat of the moment to defuse difficult situations while respecting everyone's dignity. In deciding which of these responses is best for you, it is helpful for you to actually picture various situations in which your child may say or do something that you consider to be inappropriate. Then try in your own mind to practice using the sentence or sentences that best fit the moment. It is sometimes necessary to do this several times before you find those that will be the best fit for you.

- I'm sorry you feel that way.
- When you calm down, I'll listen. *Take a few deep breaths.*
- I know you're very mad, but please don't talk to me that way.
- When you are ready to talk without yelling, let me know.
- I don't appreciate being talked to in that way.
- Your language is totally unacceptable. Now, what is it that you really want to say?
- I guess you and I see this differently. Let's try to find a solution later when we're both calmer.
- Now is not a good time for me to deal with this. I need to calm down and then we'll talk.
- You are just not yourself today so I am going to let that slide right now rather than get into a hassle about it.

Either immediately after the event or after you or the child calms down, ask, "What's really bothering you?"

## USE EXAGGERATION AND PARADOX

You may often be able to defuse oppositional behavior, such as when a child says, "No!"; "You can't make me!"; or "I'm not going to_____!" with an element of humor. Exaggerate your child's refusal in a playful way. For example:

> *Parent:* Eli, please eat your vegetables. You need to eat something healthy before dessert.

> *Eli:* I'm not going to. I hate vegetables!

The parent explains why it is important to eat vegetables, but Eli continues to refuse. Parent decides to respond with exaggeration and paradox:

> *Parent:* (pretending to be mad) YOU KNOW I DON'T THINK YOU SHOULD EAT THEM! AFTER ALL, THEY ARE DISGUSTING. I DON'T UNDERSTAND WHY ANYONE WOULD OR SHOULD EAT THEM! DON'T EVEN TRY!! AFTER ALL, THEY ARE GOOD FOR YOU. NOBODY SHOULD HAVE TO EAT ANYTHING THAT IS HEALTHY!

This usually creates enough space by changing the tone from a power struggle that can escalate to a playful moment that settles things down. Eli may still not eat his vegetables, but without threats or further discussion, there can still be no dessert (if that is the consequence).

Kids who are predictably oppositional hate doing whatever seems like a "have to," so compliance becomes more likely when they are instructed to do the opposite of what is actually required. For example, a teacher whose student *never* does homework privately tells that student that she has decided to be more respectful and will stop nagging him to do something that goes against his values (e.g., "Since I know how strongly you are against doing homework, consider tonight's assignment for everyone else but not required for you. It is about time that I respect your decisions so tomorrow if you don't have the assignment done, you will get a zero but I think it is far more important for you to do what you think is right and for me to stop bugging you about it.").

If the child shows up the next day with no homework, the teacher privately thanks him for doing as he was told. Most oppositional kids hate to comply and will be bothered by this response. As a sincerity test, many will actually do an assignment a day or two later (often well done). The teacher must refrain from expressing any enthusiasm since the child actually went against the rule by doing his homework (e.g., "Maybe you didn't understand what I said yesterday. I told you that homework was not required. Did you misunderstand? Since you did the assignment and did it well, I guess you'll have to get a decent grade, but more important is for you to do what you think is right. Keep in mind that from now on, doing assignments is completely up to you.").

In order for this strategy to work effectively:

1. Since many teachers become disgusted with students who put forth no effort, there must be an attitude of "you (student) are more important than what you do (your performance)."

2. The paradox must be presented without a hint of sarcasm.

3. The zero for non-productivity must remain (even though ineffective with the student) although presented without threat, in the event that other students want the same freedom to decide (e.g., "It's not fair that he doesn't have to do homework but I do."). Any student that challenges can be reminded that s/he always has the freedom to decide as long they are willing to accept the consequence (most students don't want zeroes).

4. The strategy must be approved by an administrator or mentor.

5. The strategy and its purpose must be satisfactorily explained to a parent(s) before being implemented (e.g., "As we both know, doing usual things like giving zeroes and taking away privileges hasn't been effective, so I'd like to try doing something really different and unusual for at least a week or two. Let me tell you what it is and see how you feel.").

## Be satisfied with the next to the last word

Too often, parents and teachers unwittingly escalate a power struggle by insisting on "having the last word." When there is anger and things are beginning to get out of hand, it is the adult that needs to act like an adult. Tough as it may be, parents are wise to practice the advice we often give our kids when other people say or do mean things to them. We often tell them to develop a thick skin and walk away ("sticks and stones").

I recall a frustrating incident with my twelve-year-old daughter that ended when I angrily told her to go to her room. As she left for her room with her back turned away from me, I could hear her annoyingly mutter, "Whatever!" At that moment, I wanted to chase after her and scold her for being ungrateful and obnoxious. Fortunately, my rational self prevailed by reminding me that she had done what I had asked (go to your room). Did she have to do it agreeably with a smile on her face? Would you? She was annoyed, but she complied. Allow that to be enough.

Have you ever muttered an expletive or secretly offered a nasty gesture at a boss while walking away after being told to do something unpleasant? You knew you were going to comply and did, but you weren't happy about it. It is the same as disgruntled and obnoxious last words or frowns from your child. It is merely a way to "save face." Be satisfied with the most effective word and that often comes next to last.

## Follow up

If necessary, meet later when everyone is calmer, and discuss more acceptable options should something similar happen again. It is often wise to revisit the incident and explore why it happened and what else you and/or your child could have done to air feelings more respectfully. Your goal should be to prevent the problem from recurring by developing a plan.

Different kids may need different ways to learn better behavior. For some, an intervention like problem solving may be sufficient, while other kids may require a more concrete consequence. The intervention should produce better behavior. In most instances, I have found it best to collaborate on an intervention with the child by asking, "Let's figure out how you could have made a better choice and how I might have handled things better, so that (yelling, swearing, blaming, etc.) when you are unhappy or feel angry doesn't happen again."

## Questions for Reflection

1. What ideas or strategies did you find most meaningful?

2. When you were a child, did you ever do things to push your parents' buttons? What did you do? Why? How did they react?

3. When your parents reacted to you, how did things usually turn out? Is there anything else you wish they had done?

4. What do your children do that pushes your buttons? How do you usually react? How would you like to react?

5. Which strategy or strategies from the examples in the chapter might keep a minor disagreement from getting worse?

## CHAPTER 10

# Helping Your Kids Handle Stress

*Your child will follow your example, not your advice.*

—Unknown

THERE IS A GROWING BODY OF RESEARCH THAT POINTS TO THE BENE-
fits of strategies like meditation and mindfulness on school performance, attention, and childhood stress (Garey, 2023). Although not everyone is sold on its benefits, and while some may not benefit, I have yet to see anyone experience ill effects from its practice. "Mindfulness" is awareness that arises by paying attention without judgment to the present moment. It temporarily puts most of the brain's higher functions to rest while it awakens our senses and calms our feelings. It is one of the main ways that you can teach your child to manage stress. As well, there are other ways we will explore in this chapter.

For various reasons, it is not uncommon for kids to internalize stress and express it through bodily aches and pains, depression, withdrawal, and sadness. Some act out aggressively while others are fidgety, showing many of the telltale signs of attention deficit hyperactivity disorder.

When I have asked youngsters to tell me what causes them stress, these are some of the responses I have heard:

- When other kids tease you by calling you names. You feel angry.
- When you're working on an arithmetic problem all morning but you can't get it right. You feel frustrated.

- When you say the wrong answer in class. You feel embarrassed.
- When you think you aren't nice looking. You worry that you won't be liked.
- When you try out for the part in the play or a spot on the team and you don't get it. You feel bad.
- When everybody seems to notice only your superstar sister. You feel jealous.
- When you have a hard time understanding stuff at school. You worry that you are stupid.
- When other kids pick on you. You are afraid you'll get hurt.
- When you can't find someone to play with or talk to. You feel lonely.
- When your parents don't get along. You worry that it is your fault.
- When you hear noises in the neighborhood that sound like gunshots. You are afraid that you or those you love will get hurt or killed.
- When nobody notices you. You feel ignored and alone.
- When kids say mean things online. You feel hurt.

Many of the strategies already shared in this book can help kids handle stress. For example, as they become better at knowing how to deal with bullying and a variety of other problems (see chapter 8) they will feel more in control and less anxious. That said, some problems lack workable solutions, and even problems with solutions that work can be stressful until they do. While it is impossible and undesirable to eliminate all sources of stress from your child's life, there are tools parents and educators can provide to keep uncomfortable feelings manageable.

There are three categories of stress-reducing methods that are easy to learn and use although most require practice for maximum effectiveness: *mind-calming* ("mindfulness"), *thought-changing*, and *acting*. A few examples follow of each, written with specific directions to assist your child. Some of these strategies were originally published as is or with modification in the author's book, *Smiling at Yourself: Educating young children about stress and self-esteem* (1991).

## Mind-calming strategies

Kids who worry a lot, who can't settle down, who are distractible or hyperactive, who have difficulty focusing their attention, or have difficulty falling asleep often find these strategies especially beneficial. There are many others easily available online that include a calming voice giving directions. Some have soft music or sounds of nature in the background. Try them yourself.

These activities require practice. At least a few minutes a few times each day is recommended, although age is a factor in determining time. At first, it is very common for most children to have difficulty staying focused so it is important to reassure them that if and when they find their mind drifting, they should simply return their attention to the activity. It is best done in a quiet spot, a comfortable chair, and with eyes closed or focused on a specific spot. You can use these exact words while guiding your child.

### 1. Deep Breathing*

One of the best and easiest ways to relax is to take some deep breaths. Here is one version. There are many others that are essentially the same as this.

a. Close your eyes as you sit in a comfortable spot, and as you breathe in through your nose, silently count from one to five.

b. When you reach five, hold your breath to the count of five.

c. Now slowly breathe out as you silently count to five.

d. After you reach five and all the air has been breathed out, count silently from one to five before you breathe in again.

e. Keep doing this: (breathe in) one . . . two . . . three . . . four . . . five; (breathe out) one . . . two . . . three . . . four . . . five; (in) one . . . two . . . three . . . four . . . five; (out) one . . . two . . . three . . . four . . . five.

*A variation is to simply count without focusing on breathing. Quietly repeat any sequence of the numbers one to five over and over. Some kids like repeating their favorite number. Either way, continue for 1-2 minutes initially.

## 2. Relax All of Yourself

a. Sit up straight in a comfortable chair with your hands in your lap and your feet on the floor. Be away from everyone. It is best to close your eyes.

b. Tense, tighten, or squeeze the muscles in your feet, legs, and toes as tightly as you can while silently counting to five.

c. Now do the same with your chest and stomach. Tighten up those muscles as you silently count to five, then release.

d. Go to your arms, fingers, and shoulders. Tighten up these muscles. Silently count to five, then let go. Feel the relaxation.

e. Now go to your head and neck. Scrunch up the muscles of your face as you count to five, then relax those muscles. Do it again, and make sure that you scrunch your mouth, nose, eyes, and teeth, each time counting to five before relaxing.

f. Now go back to your feet and do the same thing again. Squeeze or tighten each body part, count to five, then relax. When you finish, open your eyes and notice how calm your whole body feels.

## 3. Guided Pictures

Some movies we watch make us feel excited (*Batman*) while others scare us (*Friday the Thirteenth*). You can create your own movie in your mind when you want to feel relaxed. Here is an example:

> Picture in front of you a soft, fluffy, thick piece of carpet. The carpet looks so comfortable that you can now actually imagine yourself lying on it. Feel how soft, warm, and fluffy it is. As you rest on your fluffy piece of carpet, you notice that it is magical and it is about to take you on a wonderful ride. Feel yourself slowly being lifted off the ground by the magic carpet beneath you. It is so magical that it keeps you safe and supported even as it floats in the air. Feel yourself calmly floating in the air aboard your carpet. Pretty soon it will be time to land so notice how it slowly gets lower and lower, passing under the clouds and heading toward a soft landing on the ground. You and your magic carpet touch the ground just as softly as a feather would land. As you look around, you notice that the only people there are the people you like or love. You might want to say hello or give them a hug or a high five on this beautiful sunny and warm day. Stay there for another moment. As you walk away from them, you see in the distance a very shiny object, and as you get closer you see a big empty barrel with your name on it. Under your name it says, "Put all your problems inside." Spend a little time now to think of a problem that has been bothering you and put it in the barrel. Maybe it is a poor grade or something mean somebody said. Maybe it's something at home or at school. Whatever it is, put it in the barrel and say goodbye for now. Stay there another moment and add anything more to the barrel. In a few moments it will be time to leave this place and return to your magic carpet for your ride home.

> It is now time to leave, so say goodbye for now. Know that you can return another time or as often as you want to this place on your own. Now get back on your magic carpet and once again feel it lift off as it did before—slowly, calmly, and safely. Above the ground, up and through the clouds you float. Notice how you begin to get closer and closer to home (our school) as you float down through the clouds. You can see your house and room (our classroom) as you get closer and closer. You are now home (here) safely. Your ride has come to an end

for now, but realize that you can return again and again. Whenever you feel ready, open your eyes. Continue to enjoy the peaceful feeling of relaxation and notice how calm, quiet, yet alert you are.

## THOUGHT-CHANGING STRATEGIES

How we think affects the way we feel. Some youngsters suffer from anxiety because of faulty thinking that spirals. Some are regularly traumatized by events over which they lack control. Others focus on the few clouds in the sky rather than the bright sunshine. Symptoms may include seeking constant reassurance, avoiding particular situations, excessive worrying about making mistakes and not measuring up especially in academic or athletic situations, and focusing much more on bad things that might happen but rarely do. Unfortunately, reasoning and logical explanations rarely work. For example, a child who won't participate aloud in class might think:

*Child:* If I speak, I might make a mistake and I hate making mistakes.

*A reassuring parent or educator might say:* Mistakes are an important part of learning. Everyone makes mistakes.

*Child:* I know.

*Parent/Educator:* So if you make a mistake what are you afraid might happen?

*Child:* The other kids would think I'm stupid.

*Parent/Educator:* But you are one of the top students in class.

*Child:* I know, but I don't want them to laugh at me.

*Parent/Educator:* Would all the kids laugh and make fun of you?

*Child:* (getting annoyed) I don't know. I don't want to talk about this anymore!

The strategies that follow provide examples of ways to help your child use her thoughts to protect herself from getting overwhelmed by life's sometimes difficult challenges. Most youngsters can learn how to correct their faulty thinking and excessive worrying.

## 1. Use Positive Self-Talk

Nobody's life is always smooth. When it gets bumpy, we can help ourselves by talking to ourselves in more helpful, positive ways. Here are some examples:

a. If someone's parents were getting divorced, would it be better to think: "My parents are getting divorced. If I had behaved better I bet they would have stayed together." *Or* "My parents are getting divorced but kids can't control what grown-ups do. I feel sad and scared and I wish they weren't but I know it is not my fault."

b. "Nobody picked me to be a partner because nobody likes me." *Or* "I wasn't picked this time so I'll work alone and I'll pick a partner next time."

c. "Writing is hard for me so I guess I just won't do the work and fail." *Or* "Writing is hard for me so I will need to get better by spending more time practicing my writing even though I'd rather be doing other things."

d. "If my brother was nicer, we wouldn't get into so many fights and I wouldn't get into trouble." *Or* "Instead of waiting for my brother to be nicer, I'll be nice first and if he is still mean, I'll ignore him or ask Mom for help."

## 2. Reward Yourself

a. With your child, brainstorm all of the things s/he enjoys doing and write them down. The list may look like:

- Watching a favorite television show
- Taking a bike ride or going on a walk
- Talking to friends
- Having ice cream
- Taking a nap
- Hanging out with a friend
- Listening to music
- Playing video games
- Spending time on a hobby
- Having a sleepover
- Playing sports

b. Either alone or with your assistance, have your child identify an important goal to achieve that takes effort (e.g., "I'm not going to get out of my seat at school today without permission more than three times."; "I will put my things away right after dinner.").

c. When a difficult goal is achieved (e.g., things are put away after dinner each day for a week), suggest s/he celebrate with a reward from the list.

d. Point out that often the best reward is to just remind oneself to feel good inside for having met a challenge or acted responsibly by silently thinking *good job* or by looking at yourself in a mirror while thinking, *I did it!*

## 3. Be Your Own Best Friend

a. Some kids obsess about mistakes and problems. Focus your child on forgiving or soothing himself as he might his best friend. Ask your child what s/he says or does to help friends when they feel sad or make mistakes. Most friends try to say or do things like:

- "You'll do better next time."
- "Everybody makes mistakes."

- "Nobody is perfect.
- "I don't always do my best either.
- "Some problems are hard to solve.
- "Don't worry about it."
- "Let's talk about it."
- "It's not your fault."
- Give a hug or change the topic to a more pleasant one
- Share a favorite snack

b. Talk to your child about forgiving and reassuring herself when s/he makes a mistake (e.g., "How would it be if you substituted one or more of these sayings [above] whenever you start thinking 'I'm stupid?' Try it. It's at least as important to be kind to yourself as you would be to a friend.").

c. Have regular conversations about things that matter. For most kids of this generation, screens with short text messages and acronyms are their primary mode of communication. This is why it has become incumbent upon caring adults to bring up topics with children about matters of concern that they may otherwise try to hide. Rarely will a teenager open up to parents or teachers with their troubled emotions until they know we will listen with love and without judgment to the things that matter most.

### 4. Ask "Mind-Shift" Questions If Your Child Temporarily Loses Control

When a child is highly provoked or out of control, we can help the child regain control by asking "mind-shift" questions. Mind-shift questions are completely unrelated to whatever might be the source of an agitated state. For example, if a child is having a tantrum, you might ask, "What did you have for breakfast today?" The question is designed to get the child less aroused and refocused. Typically, the child will pause the outburst momentarily and say, "Why are you asking me that?" You can then say,

"Because now I have your attention. Before, you were too mad to listen. So what did you have for breakfast today?"

Any personally neutral question (or comment) can serve the mind-shift function. Questions with a food theme are often effective. Other possibilities are:

- What's on TV tonight?
- Who won the game?
- Do you like Coke or Pepsi? Cowboys or Giants? Blue, Red, or Orange?
- Who's the best: Superman, Black Panther, or Wonder Woman?
- Which basketball team do you want to play for someday?
- What are you going to do when you calm down?

## ACTING STRATEGIES

Just about everybody knows that when we feel happy, we smile, laugh, and act friendly. But did you know that if you aren't happy and you smile, act friendly and laugh, you can make yourself feel happier? That's right. You don't have to wait to feel a certain way in order to act a certain way. There are times when the best way to change how you feel is to act how you want to feel. Parents and educators are encouraged to try these next few activities and see for yourself. Then share them with your child.

## SMILING

1. Look into a mirror and put a happy smile on your face. It might help for you to think of something funny that has happened in the past that made you smile from your teeth to your toes.

2. Notice yourself smiling into the mirror as you think about this funny thing.

3. Every day before you get out of bed or before you fall asleep at night (or both), close your eyes and picture in your mind that happy

smiling face from the mirror looking at your eyes. Very slowly let that smiling face move itself down to your mouth. Now let the smile work itself all the way through your throat and into your stomach. Notice how your stomach begins to feel as if it tickles wants to laugh. Keep looking at that smiling face from the mirror and move all the way through your stomach, to your legs, ankles, and toes. You begin to feel sparkly all over your body from the top of your head to the tips of your toes.

4. Keep enjoying this happy feeling. . . . Whenever you want, open your eyes and realize how much power you have to make yourself feel good.

5. The next time you are in a grouchy mood, whether at home, school, or at a family visit, try smiling at yourself.

## LAUGHING ON PURPOSE

I recall driving my daughter and a friend to the mall when they were about twelve years old. They were both in dreary moods that matched the gloomy weather outside.

Deciding to try to change the mood, I explained how it was often possible to make ourselves feel better by laughing. I had discovered this quite by accident after reading an article about it in a casual magazine. About a week later, I was having a day filled with numerous responsibilities and lots of stress. I went into my office, closed the door, and instead of letting off steam in ways that I had done many times before, I forced myself to laugh as if I were watching either an Amy Schumer or Jim Gaffigan routine, two of my favorite stand-up comedians. It worked!!

Anyway, both girls seemed to think the idea was ridiculous, but undeterred and ignoring their skepticism and initial silence, I forced myself to laugh from the belly up. For the first several seconds, I was the only one, but as I laughed harder and harder, they both started giggling and before long we were all laughing uncontrollably. Needless to say, the mood changed dramatically! Now adults, when these young women get together, they have fun recalling that experience.

Laughter can help prevent disease, prolong life, and reduce stress. Laugh with your child. Encourage them to laugh on their own. As silly as it might sound, there are actually "laughter clubs," where adults meet, sometimes outdoors, and practice deep laughter together. Many pair laughter with yoga or meditation. If necessary to get started, try imagining funny scenarios: your mother serving dinner while she is walking on her hands; a teacher or boss blowing a big bubble and it exploding all over his face; your friend talking as ink runs down the side of her mouth and she doesn't know it.

Instead of laughter being viewed as a classroom disruption warranting discipline, teachers might consider setting aside some classroom time for laughter as the main activity or as a strategy to channel the giggles.

## QUESTIONS FOR REFLECTION

1. The following are a few sayings and thoughts I have learned over the years that relate to stress. There are many others in books and online. What do these mean to you? How might you best share them with your child?

- Give your stress wings and let it fly away.
- "The greatest weapon against stress is our ability to choose one thought over another."—William James
- In a year you'll barely remember why you felt so stressed, so why stress about it now?
- Worrying does not take away tomorrow's troubles; it takes away today's peace.

2. Which strategies from the three stress-reducing methods mentioned in the chapter do you think your child might derive the most benefit from?

3. Kids often model what they see. What are some positive and negative ways that you currently handle stress?

4. All of the suggested strategies can benefit adults as well as children. As you think about each, how might you benefit if you practiced it regularly?

5. How might you emphasize the importance of laughter in your home or classroom?

# CHAPTER 11

# Take Good Emotional Care of Yourself

*In our happiest of childhood memories, our parents were happy too.*
—ROBERT BRAULT

BEFORE BIRTH, MOST EXPECTANT PARENTS ARE FILLED WITH EXCITE-
ment about the endless possibilities this new life will bring. And there is
much to be excited about! We imagine a new cute, little cuddly being and
can't wait to meet her or him. Hopes and dreams spring eternal. When
s/he finally arrives, we instantly fall in love with this totally sweet, yet
entirely dependent person. Heightening our joy are the gifts and congratulations offered by others. We delight in watching our adorable, yet
helpless infant pass through many developmental stages and phases. We
worry about his or her needs and plan for her future.

Some of us get temperamentally difficult kids who fuss from their
first day of life, while others have to deal merely with the normal ups
and downs that everyday living brings. All of us need to expend tons of
our energy in looking after and guiding our children although by and
large much of what we worry about as our children grow is minor and
mostly unimportant in the long run. It took me until my third child to
realize this.

Since there is nothing more important than our children, it is vital
to take good emotional care of ourselves so we have the energy to deal
with the myriad challenges they bring along the way. There are numerous
strategies within this book, particularly in the prior chapter that can be

as effective for you as they are for your child. In addition to these, a few more follow:

## LET OFF STEAM SAFELY

All parents get frustrated and angry. Although most have a hard time admitting it, it is entirely normal from time to time to strongly dislike something your child says or does. In virtually all families, there is often one child in particular who is more likely to drive you crazier than the others. Neither may be at fault, but as the parent you need to remain the adult. To stay sane, take some time to let off steam. Instead of yelling, withdrawing, or feeling guilty, before you react try to remove yourself from a frustrating situation.

In the privacy of a room, the car, or some other temporary sanctuary, imagine your frustrating child is there and let them know how you feel. Don't hold back. S/he is not really there, so release all of your bottled-up emotion. It might help to scream into a pillow or punch a punching bag. Sometimes we need to safely release pent-up emotions to think more clearly.

## WORRIES WORTH THE WORRY

Most things we worry about never happen. And most of the things worth worrying about are beyond our control. For one week, each time you find yourself worrying about something, write it down on a separate piece of paper and put it in a shoe box or some other storage box. If you prefer, just list each worry. If there is really something you can do to prevent your worry from happening, do it.

At the end of the week, read each of the worries you wrote. Make two piles. One has all the things you worried about that caused you tension but did not actually happen, while the other has things that did happen. Which pile has more? It can be useful to realize what is worth worrying about and what isn't. Continue doing this for the next three weeks, except be sure to read the "worth worrying about" pile from each prior week. If you are no longer worrying about an item on any of the prior weeks' lists, remove it. At the end of the month, develop a plan to deal with those that remain in the "worth worrying about" pile and let the rest go.

## TAKE TIME FOR YOURSELF

Try to enlist grandparents or find a babysitter early on and get away for an hour or two a few times each week if possible. If not, are there other parents in your situation who might watch your kids for a portion of a day while you watch theirs another day?

Shop, get a manicure, go to the spa, see a movie, or read a book. Get with your partner or a friend and go out to dinner or play a game. No matter how busy you are raising your child and/or working at your out-of-home job, you need and deserve to make time for yourself to relax and enjoy.

If you are an educator, are there older students from upper grades who might provide a little relief by spending some class time tutoring or taking a walk with a disruptive student? Are there any colleagues you could lean on who might be able to cover some or all of a class for you while you do one or more of the activities below?

Nurturing yourself will enable you to better care for your child. Here are a baker's dozen plus one ideas that can take less than five minutes:*

1. Move (e.g., take a brisk walk; run in place; put in the ear pods and turn up the music and dance).

2. Give yourself three compliments in the morning and three in the afternoon.

3. Get some sweet-smelling flowers or fragrances and inhale.

4. Squeeze a stress ball.

5. Get a handheld massager and use it.

6. Close your eyes and meditate for a few minutes.

7. Call a friend—do a one-way "let off steam"—take a few deep breaths.

8. Stick your head outside for a breath of fresh air.

9. Do a few items on a crossword puzzle.

10. Give yourself a hug. Wrap your arms around yourself and hug yourself as you would a friend in need.

11. Force a belly laugh that lasts at least 30 seconds.

12. Forgive yourself if you start beating yourself up by saying to yourself, "I am doing the best I can right now. I will get through this moment (day). I just need another moment to regroup."

13. Notice any and all negative emotions. Acknowledge them briefly, then put them on an imaginary cloud and let them float away.

14. 14. Put a bit of honey or a square of chocolate in your mouth and let it sweeten the moment.

*Some of these activities appear in the author's publication, *The Resilient Teacher*

## BUILD A SUPPORT GROUP

Try to build or join a support group with other parents who are at a similar stage of life so you can share common joys and frustrations. Within the group, there may be others you can turn to between meetings. Educators should more regularly seek possible solutions from each other to problems they may be having with students, colleagues, parents, or demands they consider unreasonable.

## QUESTIONS FOR REFLECTION

1. Make a list of things you like to do that take 10 minutes or less and do at least one of those activities every day.

2. Are there non-judgmental people you can talk to when you need a listening ear? Contact one or more when you feel a need to talk or are seeking perspective from someone else.

3. What are some healthy ways to let off steam when frustrated?

4. Are there activities you used to enjoy that you no longer do because of your schedule or responsibilities? Can you return to at least one of these activities? If you cannot give the time and attention to it as you once did, consider how your life might be enriched if you participated in that activity less rather than not at all.

5. If your anger and/or frustration is getting the better of you, seek out professional help. While it is sometimes difficult for an individual to admit that they need help, it is better to seek help *before* saying or doing something you may later regret!

# CHAPTER 12

# Conclusion

*When my mom told me, "you're a great mom."*

—Charlize Theron


*When my own mother said I had become an incredible parent.*

—Julia Roberts


*I'm always really touched when my mother tells me that I'm a good mother. . . . Her compliment holds a lot of value in my life.*

—Reece Witherspoon


*The first time my mom told me that she thought I was a good mother.*

—Kerri Washington


*You have really happy children . . . well done!*

—Melissa McCarthy

*When the flight attendants say to me, "You have the most well-behaved children of anyone on my plane." Honestly, I've never felt so much feeling from a compliment in my life.*

—GWYNETH PALTROW

THE RESPONSES ABOVE FROM CELEBRITIES (*PEOPLE*, UPDATED APRIL 25, 2022) were to the question, "What's the most beautiful thing anyone has ever said to you?" Although there can be little doubt that each of these widely admired women has received numerous compliments from adoring fans, the most meaningful has to do with their parenting, often from their own parent(s). Perhaps that is because it is easier to do almost anything else than it is to parent. Yet there is no greater payoff. The same can be said for teachers, but too often teachers never get to see what became of their students. Below are the quotes of a few celebrities about teachers who made a powerful difference in their lives:

*One of the most important women in my life.*

—COLIN FIRTH ACKNOWLEDGING PENNY EDWARDS, ONE OF
HIS TEACHERS

*It can be the difference between, literally, life and death—like a kid who lives a successful life and a kid who punks out in the gutter.*

—JON HAMM, REFERRING TO TEACHERS FOR GUIDING THE
TRAJECTORY OF HIS LIFE AFTER HE LOST HIS PARENTS

*She believed in not only us, but a lot of students. . . . Some of the students that had a tough time, she never gave up on them. That's what I loved about her. It takes a lot to stay motivated and not become jaded as a teacher because you so often see so many cases you can't help. But she never thought of it that way.*

—VENUS WILLIAMS, REFERRING TO SANDRA MCMANUS

FOR PARENTS AND EDUCATORS, OUR CHILDREN ARE OUR LEGACY. WRIT-
ers and thinkers from Dr. Spock to Dr. Phil have offered thousands of
strategies, suggestions, and guidelines. Still, caregivers often wonder if
they are doing the right thing. As our children get older, the problems
become more perplexing. Crying for milk evolves into nagging for video
games which turns into rolling their eyes in embarrassment when we
speak. Just as it is with most of us, whatever wisdom we have remains
largely undiscovered until they become parents themselves.

So the ideas offered in this book are done so with humility. There
have been many times in my own parenting and teaching when I strug-
gled to use the very same strategies I have shared in this book. My now
adult son still gets a kick out of occasionally reminding me of the time he
was in sixth grade, and I lost my temper and started yelling and whacking
him with a pillow out of sheer exasperation at his dismissive indifference
when his teacher called home for the third time complaining about his
behavior. Shortly after, I remember him pulling one of the books I wrote
on classroom discipline and pointing to the page that said, "Scolding,
yelling, and hitting were inappropriate, ineffective, and undignified ways
of correcting behavior." To this day, I remain humbled by that moment
(and others) as a helpful reminder each time I lapse into expecting perfection from my own children or myself.

Parent each day with as much love, guidance, and joy as you can.
Revel in your child's growth. Celebrate their achievements, respect their
thoughts, and correct their errors.

Right before an important event in the lives of my twin teen grandchildren ending with a party that required much planning with a lot of
moving parts, one of my sons came to my house, sat down, and exhaust-
edly exclaimed, "Some days being a parent is the most draining job on
earth!" In that moment, I totally understood but I couldn't help but
remember the emptiness I felt when leaving him at college a thousand
miles away or sobbing the first time I walked into my youngest child's
room after she moved away, her scent still fresh on the pillow.

I end with a writing (Wet Oatmeal Kisses) attributed to the late brilliant journalist and humorist Erma Bombeck about what our lives might
look like when our kids are grown and on their own:

*ONE OF THESE DAYS YOU'LL EXPLODE AND SHOUT TO ALL THE KIDS,*

*"WHY DON'T YOU JUST GROW UP AND ACT YOUR AGE!"*

*AND THEY WILL . . .*

*OR, "YOU GUYS GET OUTSIDE AND FIND SOMETHING TO DO—WITHOUT HURTING EACH OTHER. AND DON'T SLAM THE DOOR!"*

*AND THEY DON'T.*

*YOU'LL STRAIGHTEN THEIR BEDROOMS UNTIL IT'S ALL NEAT AND TIDY, TOYS DISPLAYED ON THE SHELF, HANGERS IN THE CLOSET, ANIMALS CAGED. YOU'LL YELL, "NOW I WANT IT TO STAY THIS WAY!"*

*AND IT WILL . . .*

*YOU WILL PREPARE A PERFECT DINNER WITH A SALAD THAT HASN'T HAD ALL THE OLIVES PICKED OUT AND A CAKE WITH NO FINGER TRACES IN THE ICING AND YOU'LL SAY, "NOW THIS IS A MEAL FOR COMPANY."*

*AND YOU WILL EAT IT ALONE . . .*

*YOU'LL YELL, "I WANT COMPLETE PRIVACY ON THE PHONE. NO SCREAMING, DO YOU HEAR ME?"*

*AND NO ONE WILL ANSWER.*

*NO MORE PLASTIC TABLECLOTHS STAINED. NO MORE DANDELION BOUQUETS. NO MORE IRON-ON PATCHES. NO MORE WET, KNOTTED SHOELACES, MUDDY BOOTS OR RUBBER BANDS FOR PONYTAILS. IMAGINE . . . A LIPSTICK WITH A POINT, NO BABYSITTERS FOR NEW YEAR'S EVE, WASHING*

*CLOTHES ONLY ONCE A WEEK, NO PTA MEETINGS OR SILLY SCHOOL PLAYS WHERE YOUR CHILD IS A TREE, NO CAR POOLS, BLARING STEREOS OR FORGOTTEN LUNCH MONEY. NO MORE CHRISTMAS PRESENTS MADE OF LIBRARY PASTE AND TOOTHPICKS, NO WET OATMEAL KISSES, NO MORE TOOTH FAIRY, NO MORE GIGGLES IN THE DARK, SCRAPED KNEES TO KISS OR STICKY FINGERS TO CLEAN ONLY A VOICE ASKING, "WHY DON'T YOU GROW UP?"*

*AND THE SILENCE ECHOES: "I DID."*

Our children won't be kids forever so savor and appreciate them while we have the greatest influence.

# Appendix A

## Conversation Starters

1. What is the funniest thing that happened today?

2. What was the most enjoyable thing you learned today?

3. What was the most boring thing you had to do today?

4. What is the best thing that has happened to you so far today?

5. If you were the teacher, is there anything you would do differently?

6. If you were in charge of getting the food at your school, what would you keep and what would you get rid of?

7. If you had to trade places for a day with somebody, who would it be?

8. What's the worst thing someone did today? Did they get in trouble?

9. What was the nicest thing you saw someone do today?

10. What was the nicest thing your teacher said or did today?

11. If you could change one rule, how would you make it be different?

12. If you could add a rule, what would it be?

13. Which kids do you most respect?

14. How is bullying handled at school?

15. If you could have been anywhere else today, where would it have been?

16. If someone was asked to tell what they liked best about you, what do you think they would they say?

17. What was the weirdest thing you saw or heard today?

18. What was the coolest outfit you saw someone wear today?

19. What's the hardest thing about school?

20. If you had to give a two-minute speech to your whole class and tell them what you like best and least, what would you say?

21. What was the best discussion you heard or had today?

22. If you didn't have to go to school, what would you do instead?

23. What do you think kids should do if they feel disrespected by an adult either at school or somewhere else?

24. Do you think if kids break a rule, they should all get the same consequence(s) even if it works well with one kid but not with another?

25. What are some of the cleverest ways kids cheat?

26. If you could design a perfect school, how would you make it?

27. When you woke up this morning, what were you most looking forward to? Did things turn out well?

28. Which do you think is worse: acting bad or feeling stupid?

29. Do you ever wonder why some kids at school or in the neighborhood seem unhappy?

30. What's something you plan to do better tomorrow than you did today?

31. What do you think it means to be *kind*?

32. What do you think it means to have *integrity*?

33. What do you think it means to be *respectful?*

34. What do you think it means to be *responsible?*

35. What do you think it means to have *self-control?*

36. Which kids seem able to get along well with everybody?

37. What is the bravest thing you have done or seen?

38. Who's the funniest kid in your class? What does he/she do?

39. Why do most parents think it is important for their kids to do well in school?

40. What makes it challenging to sometimes concentrate or pay attention?

41. On a scale of 1 to 10, with a 10 being the "best," how would you rate your teacher?

42. On a scale of 1 to 10, with a 10 being the "happiest," how would you rate today?

43. On a scale of 1 to 10, with a 10 being really smart, how smart did you feel today?

44. On a scale of 1 to 10, with a 10 being the most "popular," how popular would you say you are with other kids?

45. If you could give your school a new name that would tell everyone what it is like to go there every day, what name would you choose?

46. If you had to pick one kid who you think will be successful when he/she gets out of school but isn't a very good student right now, who would you choose? Why?

47. Is there anything you think I should have apologized about but I haven't?

48. Would you rather be the smartest kid in a regular class or an average kid in a gifted class?

49. What is your favorite song (video game)? What's it about?

50. If you could hang out with any three people in the world, who would you choose?

51. Is there anyone you feel you can really tell everything to about yourself, including your fears, worries, and mistakes?

52. Can you think of some ways I can be a better parent for you?

53. If you had a hundred (thousand; million) dollars to spend, but you had to spend it on making the world a better place, how would you spend the money?

54. What is one thing your friends don't know about you?

55. Other than me (smile on your face), which of your friends has the best parent(s)? Why?

56. If you could actually be a superhero like Superman, Batman, Spiderman, Wonder Woman, and others, who would you choose?

57. Would you rather be the best player on a lousy team or an okay player on a really good team?

58. Can you name one or two things you'd like us to do more of as a family on the weekend? Less of?

59. If you could keep one thing the same forever, what would it be?

60. If someone could trade places with you for at least one day, what do you think they would most like about being you?

61. What would you buy for yourself if you had all the money in the world?

62. What's the best excuse you've ever heard? What's the worst excuse?

List other questions you could ask your child to start a conversation.

# Bibliography and Resources

Blakely, Bridget F. (2017). *Anxiety Relief for Kids.* Oakland, CA: New Harbinger Press.

Borba, M. (2022). *Thrivers: The Surprising Reasons Why Some Kids Struggle and Others Shine.* New York: G. P. Putnam's Sons.

Borba, M. (1999). *Parents Do Make a Difference.* San Francisco: Jossey-Bass.

Bouchrika, I. (2022). *Does It Matter Where You Go to College? It Depends on Who You Are.* https://research.com/universities-colleges/does-it-matter-where-you-go-to-college

Chaarani, B., et al. (2022). Association of Video Gaming with Cognitive Performance among Children (link is external). JAMA Open Network. DOI: 10.1001/jamanetworkopen.2022.35721

Curwin, R., Mendler, A., & Mendler, B. (2018). *Discipline with Dignity, 4th Edition.* Alexandria, VA: ASCD Arias.

Faber, Adele, & Mazlish, Elaine. (2012) *How to Talk so Kids Will Listen and How to Listen so Kids Will Talk, Thirtieth Anniversary Edition.* New York: Simon & Schuster.

Garey, J (2023). "The Power of Mindfulness: How a Meditation Practice Can Help Kids Become Less Anxious, More Focused." childmind.org (February 10, 2023).

Ginott, H. (1965). *Between Parent and Child.* New York: MacMillan.

Hoerr, T. R. (2013) *Fostering Grit: How Do I Prepare My Students for the Real World?* Alexandria, VA: ASCD Arias.

Maata, P. (2023). Writing Down Goals Statistics, Facts and Trends in 2023. Last updated: March 23, 2023. https://dreammakerr.com.

McMahon, S. D., Anderman, E. M., Astor, R. A., Espelage, D. L., Martinez, A., Reddy, L. A., & Worrell, F. C. (2022). Violence Against Educators and School Personnel: Crisis During COVID. Technical Report. American Psychological Association.

Mendler, A. (2021). *Motivating Students Who Don't Care: Proven Strategies to Engage all Learners.* Alexandria, VA, Association for Supervision and Curriculum Development.

Mendler, A. (2014). *The Resilient Teacher.* Alexandria, VA: ASCD Arias.

Mendler, A., & Mendler B. (2012). *Power Struggles, 2nd Edition.* Bloomington, IN: Solution Tree.

Mendler, A. (1991). *Smiling at Yourself: Educating Young Children About Stress and Self-Esteem.* Santa Cruz, CA: ETR Associates.

Peri, C. (2011). *Teenagers Educated the Village Way*. Englewood, NJ: Values Network Publishing Group.

Price, L. (2022). "Stars Share the Most Beautiful Thing Anyone Ever Said to Them." People.com (updated April 25, 2022).

Quealy, K., & Miller, C. C. (2019). "Young Adulthood in America: Children Are Grown but Parenting Doesn't Stop." *New York Times*, March 13, 2019.

Stock, G. (2004). *The Kids' Book of Questions*. New York: Workman Publishing Co.

Turnbridge (2022). "The Importance of Talking to Kids about Drugs." https//turnbridge .com

University of Notre Dame. "Degrees of happiness? Formal Education Does Not Lead to Greater Job Satisfaction." ScienceDaily, March 30, 2021. www.sciencedaily.com/ releases/2021/03/210330121213.htm

Wooden, J., with Tobin, J. (2003). *They Call Me Coach: 2nd Edition*. New York: McGraw Hill.

Zalewski, S. (2020) "Game on! Video games as a counseling tool." *ACAC Newsletter*, 7(2), 17–19.

# Index

# About the Author

**Allen N. Mendler**, PhD, is an educator and school psychologist who resides in Rochester, New York. He has developed effective frameworks and strategies for educators, youth professionals, and parents to help youth with learning and behavior problems succeed. Dr. Mendler has given many workshops and seminars to professionals and parents and is highly acclaimed as a motivational speaker and trainer for numerous educational organizations on topics pertaining to challenging students. Allen is the author or co-author of twenty books and many publications including all editions of the iconic *Discipline with Dignity*, *Connecting with Students*, *Power Struggles*, and *Motivating Students Who Don't Care*. His books and articles have been translated into several languages including Arabic, Chinese, Dutch, Korean, Spanish, Slovene, and Polish. In his spare time, he plays guitar and sings to himself (not very well), and plays violin (better) with a few community orchestras. His favorite pastime is doing things, going places, and hanging out with his grandchildren.

www.ingramcontent.com/pod-product-compliance
Lightning Source LLC
Chambersburg PA
CBHW020613270326
41927CB00005B/312